MYRTLEFIELD

HOUSE

Christianity
Opium or Truth?

Myrtlefield Encounters

Myrtlefield Encounters are complementary studies of biblical literature, Christian teaching and apologetics. The books in this series engage the minds of believers and sceptics. They show how God has spoken in the Bible to address the realities of life and its questions, problems, beauty and potential.

Christianity
Opium or Truth?

David Gooding

John Lennox

Myrtlefield Encounters

Cover design: Ben Bredeweg.
Cover photo: © Alan Lesheim. Used by permission.

First published 1992. Originally published as a series of articles in the Russian newspaper, *Uchitelskaya Gazeta*. Chapter 7 was previously published in *The Bible and Ethics*.
Second English edition, revised and enlarged, 2014

Published by The Myrtlefield Trust, 180 Mountsandel Road, Coleraine, N Ireland, BT52 1TB
w: www.myrtlefieldhouse.com
e: info@myrtlefieldhouse.com

ISBN: 978-1-874584-53-7 (pbk.)
ISBN: 978-1-874584-54-4 (PDF)
ISBN: 978-1-874584-55-1 (Kindle)
ISBN: 978-1-874584-56-8 (EPUB without DRM)

17 16 15   10 9 8 7 6 5 4 3 2

Contents

CHAPTER 1

Christianity: opium
of the people?

It was undoubtedly genuine compassion for the poor
that led Karl Marx to declare: 'Religion is the sigh of the
oppressed creature, the heart of a heartless world, and the
soul of soulless conditions. It is the opium of the people.' In
so saying Marx was not merely criticizing false religion. The
Bible itself is no less rigorous than Marx in denouncing false
religion that connives at heartless capitalists who oppress
their workers (see, e.g. Jas 2:6-7; 5:1-6). Marx was indicting
all religion on the ground that the workers took it like
an opiate which dulled their pain with delusory promises
of heaven and so made them passively tolerate injustice
instead of actively struggling against it. Although Marxism
has largely gone out of fashion among theoreticians of economic thought, and even more so in economic practice, it is
worth considering its criticisms of religion. For many today
would still agree with its basic diagnosis—that religion is a

kind of disease, a debilitating condition that keeps humanity[1] from reaching its full potential.

The Marxist cure was first to jettison all religion and then, starting with man as man in the spirit of true humanism, to set about the formation of a 'new man'. In 1961, the Communist Party of the USSR stated:

> The moulding of the new man is a long and complicated process. . . . Communist education presupposes the emancipation of the mind from the religious prejudices and superstitions that still prevent some Soviet people from displaying their creative ability to the full. A more effective system of scientific atheist propaganda is needed, one that will embrace all sections and groups of the population, and will prevent the dissemination of religious views, especially among children and adolescents. Nor must it be forgotten that the survivals of capitalism in the minds of people have to be overcome and a new man educated under conditions of a fierce ideological struggle.[2]

Interestingly enough the New Testament agrees with Marxism, in this particular at least, that religious rituals and disciplines and moral effort are all insufficient: nothing avails except the creation of a 'new man' (see 2 Cor 5:17; Eph 2:8–10; 4:22–24). Of course, Marxism and Christianity will disagree over what is wrong with the 'old man', over what kind of 'new man' is desirable, and over the means of

1 In this book we use the terms 'humanity' and 'man' interchangeably to denote the entire human race.
2 *Documents of 22nd Congress of the CPSU*, 1:176–78.

introducing the 'new man'. But more of that later. For the moment let us return to the question of opium.

If it is true that in some centuries and in some countries religion has acted like a sedative, it is also true that in this century and the last humanistic philosophies, both of the right and of the left, have acted like powerful stimulants. Their promises of a future utopia have galvanized people's innate sense of right and wrong into heroic action and sacrifice to help bring about the promised utopia. In this cause during the last century millions have died. But the promised utopia was not achieved. It seems further off than before. As far as these millions of dead people are concerned, the hopes raised in them by these humanistic philosophies, for which they gave or were robbed of their lives, have proved to be delusions.

What then shall we say about this instinctive sense of right and wrong which all of us have, which makes us feel that we have a right to justice, and which drives many people to struggle to obtain it? Obviously it was not implanted in human beings by religion, for atheists have it as keenly as believers in God. Where then does it come from? And how valid a guide is it for expecting that justice will one day triumph?

The Bible says that it has been implanted in us by God our Creator. All his divine authority stands behind it. And though in us and in our world it is often suppressed, distorted, frustrated and cheated as a result of humanity's sin and rebellion against God, it will one day be vindicated. God is going to judge this world in righteousness through Jesus Christ, and there will also be a final judgment. Justice will be done for all who have ever

3

lived on this earth (Acts 17:31; Rev 20:11–15). Here, then, is tremendous assurance. It is worthwhile striving for justice and standing against sin, evil and every kind of corruption. Our sense of right and wrong is valid: it is not an illusion.

'But no,' says humanism, 'our sense of right and wrong is not as significant as that: it is simply the product of evolutionary development.' Then there can be no guarantee that it will be satisfied in the case of any particular individual or of any particular generation! And since there is no God, and since there will be no final judgment, the millions who suffered unjustly on earth in the past, will not find justice even in the life to come, for there is no life to come. Moreover, for millions still living, the hope of justice in this life or the next will likewise prove a mocking delusion. What kind of an incentive is that for struggling for justice now, or even for some future utopia which like all those promised through history might never come anyway? It is not a stimulant. It is not even a sedative. It is a depressant.

But let us now consider the proposition that nothing avails except the formation of a 'new man'. Here the Bible would whole-heartedly agree with Marx against many forms of popular religion. The Bible teaches that man is basically evil. His heart is deceitful above all things and desperately sick (Jer 17:9). Nothing, not even the best of religious rituals or disciplines, nor even man's honest moral endeavour, can cure man's evil heart and make man acceptable to God or a fit citizen of any utopia. Nothing, that is, except the removal of man's evil heart and its replacement by a new heart, by a new spirit; in other words nothing but the creation of a new man through personal repentance

4

and faith in the crucified and risen Son of God leading to reconciliation with God, forgiveness and a new life (Ezek 36:26; Titus 3:1–7; 2 Cor 5:17; Eph 2:8–10).

Marxism, by contrast has taught that man is not basically evil, only as yet imperfect, distorted and alienated by capitalist oppression. Remove the oppression, and man will save himself and his society by his own work. But once again bitter experience has proved that this hope too is a delusion. In all centuries and right up to the present day, the very best of political and economic schemes have been, and continue to be, wrecked by man's continuing selfishness, envy, jealousy, greed, lust, drunkenness, theft, lying, cruelty, and murdering. History shows that man is, as the Bible says he is, basically sinful and evil.

How then can he be saved? Certainly not by independence of God: that is the cause of his trouble, not the cure. Nor even by religious rituals and good works. Speaking to a man who was already very religious Christ put it this way: 'That which is born of the flesh is flesh, and that which is born of the Spirit is spirit. Do not marvel that I said to you, "You must be born again."' (John 3:6–7).

You may feed, groom and train a dog, but you will never by those means turn it into a human being. To become a man, it would have to be born again. The only way of turning a fallen, sinful human being into a child of God is regeneration by the Spirit of God. Hopes of doing it by any other means are delusions.

CHAPTER 2

The Bible: myth or truth?

Perhaps some readers will be surprised that our defence of Christianity comes directly from the Bible. To some people, the Bible itself is the problem when it comes to taking seriously any of Christianity's claims to be true. Why bother with Christianity at all when it is indebted to a book that is seriously doubted by intelligent people? Let us face the question directly together.

In our experience there are varied reasons why people think the Bible cannot and should not be believed. One reason many people give is that because the New Testament during the first fifteen centuries of its existence had to be copied out by hand, with all the possibilities of mistakes and changes that that implies, we cannot be sure, so they say, when we now read it, that we are reading what its original authors wrote.

This objection is generally made by people who are not aware how overwhelmingly strong the evidence is for the original text of the New Testament. First, there is the sheer number of the manuscripts containing part or whole of the New Testament. There are over 5,000 of them. While, of course, there are copying mistakes in all those manuscripts—for it is virtually impossible to copy out a lengthy document by hand without making some mistakes—no two manuscripts contain exactly the same mistakes. And therefore by comparing all these manuscripts with each other it is possible to reconstruct the original text to a point where less than two per cent is uncertain, with a large part of that two per cent involving small linguistic features that make no difference to the general meaning. Moreover, since no New Testament doctrine depends solely on one verse or one passage, no New Testament doctrine is put in doubt by these minor uncertainties.

And then there is the great age of some of the New Testament manuscripts. A substantial part of the New Testament exists in a manuscript that was written about AD 200, and the earliest surviving manuscript containing the whole of the New Testament was written not much, if at all, later than AD 360. See what that implies. Take the manuscript that was written about AD 200. It is, itself, now nearly 1,800 years old. How old was the manuscript from which it was originally copied? We do not know, of course. But it could easily have been 140 years old; and if it was, it was written out when many of the authors of the New Testament were still alive.

A comparison will help—and here I (David Gooding) speak as a lifelong student of the ancient classical literatures. Some of the works of the very famous ancient Greek and Latin authors have come down to us in only a few, late (i.e. seventh to ninth century) manuscripts.

Yet no classical scholar would think of questioning their validity as reliable representations of what the original authors wrote. Compared with this, the evidence for the text of the New Testament is overwhelming. We may have every confidence then, that when today we read the New Testament, we have for all practical purposes what its original authors intended us to have.[1]

But, of course, the greatest difficulty by far which people have in believing the Bible is the claims it makes; particularly its claim that Jesus is the Son of God, that he is the Creator incarnate, who has visited our earth to communicate with us and to reveal God to us. Many people feel that they could not possibly believe a book that made such claims. They do not believe in the existence of a Creator anyway; and so they suppose in advance, without reading or studying the New Testament for themselves, that it cannot be describing a historical reality when it claims that Jesus was both man and God. And they fall back on the idea that the figure of Jesus Christ as described in the New Testament is the invention of the authors of the Gospels.

The character of Jesus not invented

So, for the sake of the argument, let us suppose for a moment that the authors of the Gospels, did not simply describe a Jesus who actually lived, but invented this

---

1 To examine the evidence further, see the book by F. F. Bruce, *The New Testament Documents: Are They Reliable?* For an equally helpful book on the Old Testament, see K. A. Kitchen's book, *On the Reliability of the Old Testament.*

character, taking as their raw material, perhaps, some peasant 'wise man', but freely re-constructing, adding to, shaping, exaggerating so that the result was an ideal, more than human, but fictional character who as such never existed. Let us, I say, suppose that this was how it was, and then let us work out the implications of our theory.

The first thing to say about it would be, that if the character of Jesus is a literary fiction, then what we have here is a near-miracle. We know a lot about fictional literary characters and how difficult it is to create a really convincing one. World literature is full of such characters, some well-drawn, some not so well. Now there is no denying that if Jesus is a literary fiction, he is a character that has achieved worldwide fame. To be able to create such a famous fictional character, the authors of the Gospels must have been literary geniuses of the highest order. Now literary geniuses of that rank are quite rare: one does not bump into one round every corner. But here we have four all flowering at once. Who were these men? And what kind of men were they? Well, two were fishermen, one was a low-level tax official, and the other a nondescript young man. Is it credible that all four happened to be literary geniuses of world rank?

But more. Even the most brilliant, most lifelike fictional characters remain for their readers simply that: fictional characters. They do not rise up out of the page, so to speak, take on an independent existence and become for their readers a real living person, whom they can know in the way one knows a living person, and with whom they can have a personal relationship. Understandably not! And yet this is what has happened to this supposedly fictional character, Jesus Christ. He has become for millions of people throughout more than twenty centuries a real, living, person, with whom they would claim to have a personal relationship; a person whom they love to the point of being prepared to die for, as thousands actually have. Now, you may think them idiots for feeling this way about Jesus. At this stage, I am not asking you to approve. I am simply stating the undeniable fact. And my point is this. If Jesus was in fact a fictional character invented by the authors of the Gospels, then in creating a character who for millions has become a living person worthy of love, devotion and sacrifice, those authors have achieved a literary feat unparalleled in the whole of world literature. Miracle would not be too strong a word for it. Perhaps, indeed, we ought to start worshipping them?

There are, of course, some (though remarkably few) characters in literature that strike us as real persons whom we can know and recognize. One of them is Plato's Socrates. Plato's dialogues are not only philosophical works, they are works of world-ranking literature. Yet the Socrates who appears in them has struck generation after generation of readers as a real person, whose character traits they would recognize anywhere; so much so that if they are presented with a depiction of Socrates in some apocryphal, second-rate work, they will say at once, 'No, that was not how the real Socrates would have reacted, or spoken.'[2]

But the reason why the Socrates of Plato's dialogues strikes us like that is because Plato did not invent him. He was a real, historical person, who actually lived. Plato's

---

2 Cf. C. S. Lewis, *Fern-Seed and Elephants*, 110.

picture of Socrates may be highly polished: but the person and character of Socrates were no invention of Plato's. It was the other way round. It was the impact of Socrates' character that helped to 'create' the philosopher and literary artist, Plato.

And so it is with Jesus Christ. And even more so. Though the whole world recognizes that the Socrates of Plato's dialogues was a real historical person, no one but a lunatic would claim to know him now as a real living person, or to have a personal relationship with him. People nowadays do not die for Socrates. They do for the Jesus of the New Testament! For he is not a literary or religious fiction invented by the authors of the Gospels. The Gospels describe a real historical figure who lived in Palestine in the reign of Tiberius Caesar, who died, and as Christians would say, who rose again from the dead and lives still.

Jesus: nobody's idea of a hero

But let's not move on too fast. Let's stay for a moment with the hypothesis that someone invented the character of Jesus, presented this fiction to the world, where it immediately appealed to people of widely different cultures, and was taken over as their religious ideal.

But this hypothesis falls at the very first hurdle. The more we know about the leading cultures of the time, the more it becomes clear, that if the character of Jesus had not been a historical reality, nobody would have invented it, even if they could. The Jesus of the Gospels fitted nobody's concept of a hero. Greek, Roman and Jew—all found him the very opposite of their ideal.

Take first the Jews, and not merely the Jews who were, and continued to be, hostile to Jesus, but the comparatively few who were at first his friends. They themselves tell us—and they certainly did not invent this bit—that there came a point when they abandoned him, so utterly contrary was he to what they looked for in a hero (Matt 26:47–56). Their concept of a hero was a messianic figure like the Maccabees. A strong, military type, fired with religious ideals, and prepared to fight (with the help of angelic assistance, so popular fervour believed) the imperialists who had subjugated the country and were suppressing the national religion.

But when matters came to a head between Jesus and the authorities and they came to arrest him, Jesus refused to fight, or to let his disciples fight either, and deliberately allowed himself to be arrested. At which point all his followers abandoned him in disgust: he was no hero of theirs! And many Jews, even today, especially those in Israel, feel similarly. A Jewish friend who only just managed to escape Hitler's gas chambers says frankly, 'This Jesus of yours is a weakling. He won't do as a messiah for me. My philosophy is that if someone biffs you on the nose, you biff him back!' That is how the first disciples of Jesus originally thought; and it was only the resurrection of Jesus that taught them otherwise and radically changed their ideas of what the Messiah should be.

Or take the Greeks of that time. The kind of hero that appealed to them, or at least to the thinking ones among them, was either the ideal Epicurean who carefully avoided, as far as possible, all pains and pleasure that could disturb his tranquillity or the ideal Stoic who, following a rigid rationality, subdued his emotions and met suffering and death with undisturbed self-possession. Plato's Socrates too, we remember, drank the poisoned cup with unflinching cheerfulness and equanimity.

How completely different is the Jesus of the Gospels, tormented with anguish and agony in Gethsemane until his sweat rolled down like heavy drops of blood as he pleaded with God to let him off drinking the cup that was presented to him, and crying out publicly on the cross, 'My God, why have you forsaken me?' He certainly was no one that a Greek would have recognized as a hero, no one that a Greek philosopher would have invented as an ideal to look up to.

And as for the Romans, among the philosophically inclined Stoicism was generally the most favoured creed, while the political and military men who came in contact with Jesus found him an impractical nonsense. He talked of himself as a king who had come into the world to bear witness to the truth. 'Truth? What's that?' said Pilate. Pilate's ultimate god was power (John 18:33–38; 19:1–12). Herod thought the claims of Jesus screamingly funny, and his soldiers considered a 'king' like Jesus fair game for the crudest of practical jokes (Luke 23:8-12).

The plain fact is that Jesus in the end ran counter to everybody's concept of an ideal hero, political, philosophical or religious. Nobody invented him, and nobody, even if they had invented him, would have considered for a moment that here was an ideal that would instantly appeal to the public. The greatest Christian preacher and missionary, Paul, confesses in his writings that the preaching of Jesus who was crucified, constantly struck Jews as scandalous and Greeks as sheer folly. If it had not been for the fact that Jesus rose from the dead, the first disciples would have abandoned all faith in him. The Gospels would never have been written.

Of course, as we now look back from the vantage point of two thousand years of history, things appear very different. The Romans who mocked Jesus eventually lost their great empire, and Tiberius Caesar is for the mass of people in the West a forgotten shade of history. But today multi-millions regard Jesus as the greatest king that ever lived, and live their lives in willing obedience to him.

Moreover, the principle of non-retaliation in the face of evil that he exemplified when he yielded to his enemies without fighting, and prayed for those who crucified him, has come to command the world's respect (even if not its obedience) and still challenges our insane human aggressiveness and violence. It has turned the cross from being a gallows of shame into the noblest attitude a person can adopt.

And as for the contrast between the calmness of Socrates and the dire agony of Jesus, in the face of death, and the confession of Jesus on the cross that God for a while abandoned him: it certainly shows that Jesus was no Greek philosopher. But then it points us to the fact that in the cross of Jesus something was taking place infinitely more significant than the death of a Greek philosopher. In the language of the New Testament, here was the Lamb of God bearing the sin of the world and through his suffering making it possible for our guilt to be removed.

More of that later. Here for the moment is my first major argument: if you suppose that Jesus Christ is an invented character, you have an insuperable problem on your hands to explain how the authors of the Gospels could possibly have managed to invent him, and, what is more, why they should have invented such a character anyway.

The greatest difficulty of all?

The greatest difficulty many people find in even contemplating the possibility that the New Testament could be true is its claim that Jesus is more than human, that he is God incarnate. Surely, they say, this must be superstition, which came about because people in the ancient world believed in many gods and imagined that gods quite frequently visited earth in the form of exceptional human beings.

Well, so you may think; but the facts are altogether otherwise. It is true, of course, that all nations in the ancient world believed that there were many gods, and that those gods did visit earth from time to time—that is, all nations except one. And that one exception was the Jewish nation to which the writers of the New Testament, almost to a man, belonged. They were strict monotheists. They despised the other nations for their absurd polytheism and for making gods out of their kings and heroes. To claim divine honours for anybody other than God the Creator was for them a blasphemy so serious that, according to their law, it was punishable by death. In their religious devotions in every home in the land they had for centuries been taught to recite daily as the fundamental tenet of their faith, 'Hear, O Israel: the LORD our God, the LORD is one' (Deut 6:4). People like this would never have thought for one moment of believing that Jesus of Nazareth was more than human, unless they had been compelled to do so by the sheer weight of the evidence.

Chief among that evidence was the fact that Jesus Christ himself by his actions and their implications and by his explicit statements claimed equality with God. And that leads me to confess to you that one of the strongest reasons I have for believing that Jesus is the Son of God is simply this: that he said he was! I know that sounds hopelessly naive; but before you write me off as a credulous simpleton, give me time to explain what I mean.

Suppose, one day I decided I wanted an opinion about some question to do with music. I should not consult just anybody. I should not even consult my next-door neighbour: he is a good medical doctor, but he is no musician. No, I should consult the highest teachers of music I could get hold of. If I could resurrect Bach or Beethoven, I would consult them. Naturally.

Now suppose I wanted to know not about music, but about morality. Once more I would consult the highest world-ranking experts I could find. And that would lead me of course to Jesus Christ. None ever taught a higher, purer morality. His Sermon on the Mount remains an unsurpassed standard. Check it for yourself. Try living the Sermon on the Mount for a week!

But with this I come to the point I want to make. When through the New Testament I come alongside Jesus of Nazareth, his teaching on morality, his holiness of life, expose me to myself as the sinner I am. I need no external proof that he is true at this level; I know it instinctively in my heart. But then comes the striking fact: it was this Jesus Christ whose moral teaching was flawless and whose life matched his teaching, that claimed to be equal with God.

What shall I make of his claim, or rather of the fact that it was he who made it? Shall I say that the author of the Sermon on the Mount was deliberately lying? Well, if he was, then he was the biggest hypocrite, the most despicable fraud, the most evil impostor that ever walked the earth. But it is impossible to read the Gospels carefully, and come away with the conclusion that Jesus was a deliberate fraud. If you doubt that, read the Gospels through once again yourself with this question in mind. You are surely good judges of character; you have to be, to find your way safely through this world. Exercise your judgment on Jesus. Assess his character as you find it in the Gospels. I more than suggest to you that whatever else you conclude about him, you will not conclude that he was a deliberate fraud.

But he could have been genuinely mistaken, you say, without being a deliberate fraud. But if so, think what that means. People who mistakenly think they are God, are megalomaniac lunatics! Was Jesus Christ a lunatic, then? Well, if he was, then very few people have been sane! And as for his being a megalomaniac, it is impossible to study the behaviour and words of Christ as described in the New Testament and come to any such conclusion. The Jesus who could say with conviction, 'Come unto me all you whose work is hard, whose load is heavy and I will give you rest. Take my yoke upon you and learn from me, for I am gentle and humble-hearted' (Matt 11:28–29 own trans.), was no Hitler or Mussolini! Or if he really was a megalomaniac,

God give us more megalomaniacs! For it is a simple matter of fact that Jesus Christ has been responsible for more mental health and stability than anyone else in the world. Reading his words has brought peace to millions. Faith in him and in his sacrifice has given millions release from the torture of a guilty conscience. Daily fellowship with him has for millions broken the grip of destructive habits, and given them new respect for themselves, a sense of purpose in life and freedom from the fear of death.

It was Jesus Christ, of course, who taught us that God is love. If you believe in God at all, you probably take it for granted that he is love. You might even suppose that just any person in any century could see that God is love. But in all my reading of the ancient Greek and Latin authors I have never found any writer or philosopher who claimed that God was love. All-powerful, yes; good in a detached, absolute sense, approving man's good behaviour and disapproving his evil acts. But love? Positive, warm-hearted, involved, caring, sacrificing love for mankind? No one ever thought it or taught it like Jesus Christ did nor with such heart-movingly direct statements as, for instance, 'Are not five sparrows sold for two pennies? And not one of them is forgotten before God. Why, even the hairs of your head are all numbered. Fear not; you are of more value than many sparrows' (Luke 12:6–7). Are these the words of a lunatic?

And then, of course, no one has ever personally expressed the love of God towards mankind as Jesus did by his self-sacrifice at Calvary. Thousands of noble and courageous men and women have endured torture and suffering and have eventually laid down their lives for their friends or their country, or in protest against some evil regime.

We rightly acclaim them as heroes. But we have missed the point if we suppose the New Testament is claiming no more than that Jesus Christ was a hero. What it claims for him, indeed what he claimed for himself, is unique in the history of both literature and religion. At the very beginning of his public ministry (not after his crucifixion) his official introducer, John the Baptist, announced that Jesus had come as the Lamb of God to take away the sin of the world (John 1:29); and the term he used, 'the Lamb of God', indicated that Jesus had come in order to die as a sacrifice to take away sin. Or, as the Apostle Peter later put it:

> You were ransomed . . . with the precious blood of Christ, like that of a lamb without blemish or spot. . . . He himself bore our sins in his body on the tree, that we might die to sin and live to righteousness. . . . For Christ also suffered once for sins, the righteous for the unrighteous that he might bring us to God. (1 Pet 1:18–19; 2:24; 3:18)

And that this was what Jesus Christ himself regarded as the chief purpose of his coming into the world is shown by the following fact. The night before his crucifixion he instituted a ceremony by which his followers should thereafter remember him; and it is very instructive to notice the nature of that ceremony. He did not ask that when his followers met together they should recite the story of one of his spectacular miracles. That would have suggested that the main thing about his ministry was that he was a miracle worker. Nor did he ask that they should select a portion of his moral teaching and recite it. That would have suggested that the main purpose of his life was to be a philosopher-teacher. He asked that they should take bread and wine to represent his body and blood, and eat and drink them in memory of the fact that on the cross he gave his body and shed his blood to secure for them forgiveness of sins (Matt 26:26–28).

And that the early Christians understood the chief purpose of Christ's coming into the world was to give himself for them as a sacrifice for their sins, is shown by the fact that right from the very beginning, as the records show, they were found meeting together to perform this ceremony. It lies at the very centre and heart of all that Christ claimed and stood for. And it is this self-sacrificing love of Christ that has broken down people's resistance to him, and won him the gratitude and personal devotion of his millions of followers. They all say with Paul, the Christian apostle, 'The life I now live in the flesh I live by faith in the Son of God, who loved me and gave himself for me' (Gal 2:20).

All this, however, brings us to the crux of the matter. There is a very good and obvious reason why no one else has ever claimed that he, or she, came into the world in order to die as a sacrifice for the sin of the world. To claim that, is to claim not to be a hero, or even a martyr, but to be more than human, to be God incarnate. Only one who was himself the infinite God could offer an adequate sacrifice for the sin of the whole world.

You will see this from the simple fact that if one of your friends were seriously to claim that the whole purpose for his being born into this world was to die for the sins of the world, you would probably seek out a psychiatrist for him. You would regard his claim as a sign of lunacy. And yet when Jesus Christ makes the claim—and he did make it: we have seen that it was not invented by the writers of the New Testament—it does not carry the faintest suggestion that he was a megalomaniac lunatic.

Indeed this claim of his is one of the things that convinces me that he is indeed the Son of God, for it both diagnoses what my fundamental problem as a human being is, and offers me the only acceptable solution to that problem. Let me explain.

All other religions and philosophies constantly inform me, each in its own way, that I ought to be good. That is helpful, I suppose; but it does not touch my real problem. I know already that I ought to be good. I don't need the help of religion or philosophy to tell me that! My problem is not that I don't know I ought to be good, but that times without number I have not been good. (And my neighbours, I notice, are in the same position.) And that is an enormous problem. What am I to say about my past sins? I have broken even my own standards, let alone God's. I have compromised and befouled my own values. How then can I find forgiveness? If I decide that my past sins do not after all matter, then I am saying that my values do not matter either. And if what I do does not matter, then I who am responsible for it do not ultimately matter. But suppose my values matter. And suppose God's standards matter and he will not lower them for me or anybody else. Then my sins matter. How can I find a forgiveness for my past, that does not by implication destroy my own values, my own significance, let alone everybody else's? And the same goes for you as well as me.

It is just here that Christ meets us. He claims authority to grant us forgiveness, but to do so without condoning our sin, or undercutting God's standards. He does not say that what we have done does not matter. He insists that the penalty for it be paid. But then, he explains, this is the central reason why he came to our earth: he is the God who set and insists on the penalty for sin, the God whose law we have broken and so have deserved that penalty. Yet he is the Creator who made us, and in love and loyalty to us took the burden of our sin upon himself, paid its penalty by his suffering at Calvary, thus upholding his law and our values, and yet making it possible for us to be granted forgiveness, if we will have it.

This then is exactly what I need, and you too. Christ has read our need, and met it as no one could. In this he is unique. As you face his claims, you may be sure of this: you will only have to decide this question once in your life. Nobody else has ever, or will ever, come alongside you and tell you that he is the Creator who made you and loves you, who came as God incarnate to die for you, so that you might be forgiven. Jesus Christ is the only one who ever claimed it. And his claim is so direct and so personal: he says he died for you; which means that you personally must make your individual response to him and to his claim.

The final validation of Christ's claims

The validation of Christ's claim lies ultimately in two things: the objective evidence of his resurrection, and our own subjective experience of the Holy Spirit's witness in our own hearts when, having been convinced by the objective evidence, we open our hearts to Christ and receive him personally as Saviour.

First then his resurrection: the New Testament writers all claim that the third day after he died and was buried, Jesus Christ literally, bodily, physically rose from the dead.

Perhaps, at this point, you will be saying to yourself that anyone who believes in the resurrection of Christ must already have committed intellectual suicide; for we know nowadays that miracles like the resurrection do not take place: science has shown them to be impossible.

But in actual fact we do not know any such thing, nor has science proved any such thing. And if you think it has, you are not quite as good a scientist as you might claim.

But, you protest, the laws of science show that it is impossible for a dead body to come to life again.

No they do not; in fact they could not. The laws of science are not some absolute laws which we find written up in the sky somewhere. The laws of science are descriptions, worked out by the scientists—and all honour to them: I for one applaud their efforts—of the way that the universe normally works; or rather, that little part of the universe that they have so far been able to study and understand.

But there are two things that we must consider in this connection. First, as you will know, perhaps better than I, there are cosmologists nowadays who seriously argue that there are so-called black holes in the universe, and that in those black holes the laws of physics break down; so that following the laws of physics backwards you come to a point where you can no longer work out what happened before that point, because the laws of physics no longer hold. You have reached what is called a singularity in the universe.

Now I know that not all cosmologists accept this theory; but my point is that those scientists who have suggested that there are such singularities in the universe are not accused of having committed intellectual suicide. Nor do genuine scientists take the view that the laws of physics prove in advance, before the evidence is investigated, that by definition there could not be any singularity in the universe. To be able to predict a priori that there could never be a singularity in the universe, science would first have to understand the working of every part of the whole universe in its entirety. Science has scarcely done that yet!

And secondly, we must always remember that the laws of science can only tell us what normally happens *as long as there is no interference in our world from outside.* But science, as science, cannot tell us whether in fact there has been such interference in the past or whether there will be in the future. We must go to history, not to science, to discover whether there have been such interferences in the past. Of course we all agree, Christian and non-Christian, that such interferences will have been exceedingly rare: miracles are by definition rare. To come to history, however, with your mind already made up that no miracle can ever have happened, and to refuse to investigate the evidence that sometimes miracles have happened, is not a truly scientific attitude. It is obscurantism.

In a later chapter we will consider more of the evidence for the resurrection. But consider this one point for now: if you refuse to believe in the resurrection you will have a host of historical problems on your hands, and one very large one in particular. No one can deny the existence of the Christian church. Nor can anyone deny that it did not always exist: it had a beginning. The question is: what brought it into being? What was its purpose? If you consult the New Testament, you will find all the early Christians saying with one voice, that the thing that brought the church into existence was the resurrection of Christ; and that the whole purpose for which it was brought into existence was to bear witness to the resurrection of Christ. Their early sermons are full of little else (see the Acts of the Apostles).

The first Christians were all Jews, born and bred. Their weekly holy day was the Sabbath, that is the last, the seventh day of the week. Then suddenly, as the records show, in addition to the Sabbath, they began meeting on the first day of the week in order to eat bread and drink wine in memory of Jesus. Why this change, and why the first day of the week? Because, the early Christians tell us, Jesus Christ rose from the dead on the first day of the week.

For their preaching of the resurrection of Jesus, the early Christians were severely persecuted, and some were tortured, fed to the lions and otherwise executed. If only they had been content simply to preach the Christian ethic, that people ought to love one another, no one would have persecuted them. But no, they would insist on witnessing to the fact that Jesus, executed by the authorities, was risen from the dead. And many of them died for it. Do you suppose that they died for a story which they, the early Christians, made up themselves and knew to be false?

Whatever you think of the Christian church, it exists; and unless we are going to shut our eyes to history, we must find some cause big enough to account for its birth. Things like the Christian church do not appear out of nowhere without any cause. Cut out the resurrection, and you are left with a gaping hole in history: the Christian church, and no adequate cause to account for its origin and existence.[3]

What's all this got to do with me?

Perhaps by now some of you are beginning to protest under your breath, 'What's all this got to do with me? I'm a biochemist, an engineer, a builder, a mother. I can't be expected, can I, to go poking around in ancient history like this? I've got enough to do with my own studies or work.'

Well, all I've been trying to do is to answer the question: 'Is it necessary to commit intellectual suicide to believe the Bible?' If you genuinely haven't the time to consider the evidence necessary for answering the question, that's too bad. Even so, I hope I have said enough to dissuade you from yielding to the temptation to go around saying that the claims of the New Testament are obvious nonsense. If you were to do that without having studied the evidence, it might be you who was committing the intellectual suicide!

But, of course, there's more to it than that. If the New Testament is right, Jesus Christ is the Son of God, our

3 For further reading see William Lane Craig's *Reasonable Faith*, Gary Habermas's *The Case for the Resurrection of Jesus*, and *Phenomenon of the New Testament* by C. F. D. Moule.

Creator—and that has everything to do with you and me and everybody else. If he is the Son of God, to neglect him, for whatever reason, is ten thousand times worse than intellectual suicide: it is culpable indifference towards our Maker. That is why the New Testament summons us to study the evidence with all the seriousness we can muster. We could hardly hope to understand the physics of the universe, without seriously studying the evidence supplied us by the universe itself. Then how could we get to know and to understand the universe's Creator without studying the evidence he has given us about himself with equal seriousness?

I find it not uncommon that otherwise highly intelligent academics, physicists, chemists, biologists, and so forth, are inclined to dismiss the Bible as nonsense. When in response I gently press them to say whether they've read the Bible, they retort, 'Of course we have.' When I then ask them what they think of the evidence the Bible submits for the deity of Christ, they generally reply, 'What evidence?'

I say, 'Take for instance the Gospel of John. Its author explains his purpose in writing: "These [signs] are written", he says as evidence to convince you "that Jesus is the Christ, the Son of God, and that by believing you may have life in his name" (John 20:31). This is the evidence I'm referring to,' I say; 'what do you think of it?'

And time and again I've had them reply to me, 'Ah, the Gospel of John. Well, no, I've not read that one. We only studied Mark at school.'

So here they are, learned professors in the university some of them, now in middle life, and never since they were children in school have they studied the Bible, and never have they read the Gospel of John through with an adult mind and with the seriousness with which they study their academic subjects. How they know its evidence is worthless, if they've never read it, I don't know. (How they can regard themselves as educated men and women if they've never read the Gospel of John seriously—I do not know either.) But the far more important thing at issue is this: the Gospel of John comes to us with the authority of Jesus Christ. If what it says is true, here is God our Creator trying to communicate with us, trying to talk to us personally, trying to reveal himself to us, so that through Jesus Christ we may enter into a personal relationship of faith and love with him. Not to be interested in discovering whether it is true or not; not to be interested in the possibility of hearing our Creator speak to us, might seem to indicate a strange, irrational predisposition on our part.

'But look,' my colleagues say to me, 'it's no good telling us to read the Bible, because we don't believe it. If we believed it, of course we would read it. You are asking us to begin by believing it, and so read it. Of course, if we believe it is true before we start, we shall believe everything it says. But we don't believe it, and there's no good our reading it.'

But to talk like that is silly. Of course I am not asking them, or you either, to believe the Bible before you start reading it. But I am asking them—and you—to read it, and then make up your mind whether it's true or not. After all, that's how you treat the newspapers, isn't it? You know before you start that some of the things they contain will be true, and some not. You certainly do not decide, before you read them, to believe whatever they say. But that doesn't stop you reading them. You have confidence enough in your own judgment to read what they say, to reflect on it and to make up your own mind whether it's true or not. I'm asking you to do the same with the New Testament.

And if you will, Jesus Christ himself guarantees that provided you are prepared to fulfil one condition, God will show you personally whether his claims are true or not. And the condition is this: 'If anyone is willing to do God's will'—that is, when he discovers what it is—'he will find out whether my teaching comes from God or whether I speak on my own' (John 7:17 own trans.). He will find out, because as he reads and studies and thinks about what Jesus taught, God will speak to his heart, and show him beyond shadow of doubt, that what Jesus says is true.

The trouble lies, I suspect, with the condition: 'if anyone is willing to do God's will'. We sense before we start, that if God did show us, it would carry profound implications for our way of life that we might not wish to face. So we would prefer to approach the whole thing impersonally, like we approach experiments in physics, without committing ourselves in advance to any practical implications. But we cannot treat God like that. We cannot come to the Almighty and say: 'Yes, I would like to know whether you are there or not, and whether Jesus Christ is your Son or not. Please show me. But I would like you to understand that if you reveal yourself to me, I still am not necessarily prepared to do anything you might tell me to do.' God has no time for spiritual dilettantes.

But if you are serious, and willing to do God's will when you know it, then make the experiment: read the Gospel of John seriously with an open mind; and Jesus Christ guarantees that God will show you what the truth is.

Someone will be saying, perhaps, 'My trouble is this: I don't even know whether God exists. If I made the experiment you suggest, should I not be in danger of imagining I heard God speak to me, when it was only auto-suggestion? How would I recognize God, even if he did speak to me?'

Well, let me finish by telling you a story about a miracle Jesus is said to have done (John 9). You may probably dismiss all stories of miracles as nonsense. Never mind for the moment. I appeal to it solely as an illustration.

Jesus, so the story goes, once came across a man who had been born blind, and asked him if he would like to be given sight.

Now I don't know if you have ever tried to explain to someone born blind what sight is, or what colour is like, or even to convince them that there are such things as light and colour. But it is mighty difficult! We could have well understood it, therefore, if the blind man had replied to Jesus, that he didn't know what sight was, and considered that all claims that there was such a thing as sight, to be nonsense. That, at least, is how many people react nowadays when they hear Jesus Christ say that he can give them spiritual sight; that he can give them eternal life, which is the faculty of knowing God personally (John 17:3).

Fortunately, however, the blind man said that if there was such a thing as sight he would like to have it. So Jesus Christ suggested to the man that there was an experiment he could perform, if he was willing to; and he guaranteed that if he performed it, he would receive sight.

Now the experiment Christ laid down seemed a strange experiment, as you will discover if you read the story. But the blind man was no obscurantist. He reasoned that Jesus Christ was no charlatan, nor lunatic either. If he said there was a thing called sight and that he could give it to anyone who wanted it, then it was worth making the experiment. There was nothing to lose. There was everything to gain. So he made the experiment, found by personal experience that it worked, and returned from the experiment, seeing.

I recommend a similar experiment to you. Read John's Gospel. As you read, say: 'God, I'm not sure if you exist. But if you do, and if Jesus is your Son and he can give me, as he claims, eternal life, whatever that is, speak to me, reveal yourself to me, show me that Jesus is your Son. And if you show me, I am prepared to do your will, whatever it turns out to be.'

And Christ guarantees that God will show you.

CHAPTER 3

But hasn't science made belief in God impossible?

One of the most deeply rooted myths that has shaped the thinking of people in the modern world is the idea that science has made belief in God and the supernatural both unnecessary and impossible for the thinking person. It is a very widespread and fallacious myth which unfortunately has become confused with true science in the minds of many people. Let us look at how the myth arose.

A modern myth

The common notion is that belief in God and the super-natural arose in a primitive stage of human development. Ancient man was confronted by all kinds of processes and happenings which he could not understand. On some of them, such as the growth of his crops and the fertility of his cattle, his very life depended. Others of them, thunder and lightning, storm and disease, threatened his very existence. Not understanding these processes and in awe of them, he did what a child would do: he personalized them. When the moon went into an eclipse, he imagined that a demon of some kind was trying to strangle the moon and he engaged in all kinds of religion and magic to try to chase the demon away. When it thundered, he thought it was some god speaking, and if lightning struck, he thought it was a malevolent spirit out to destroy him. He even thought that by observing any unusual phenomenon in nature he could predict what the gods were going to do. But since in more recent centuries we have developed the scientific method with ever greater sophistication, we have come to understand more and more the processes of nature. We now can see that an eclipse is not caused by a demon, nor are lightning and disease caused by malevolent spirits. We have discovered that the processes of nature are impersonal and in principle (at the non-quantum level) completely predictable. Atheists therefore argue that there is no longer any need to bring in the idea of God and the supernatural to explain the workings of nature. There is even no need to call God in to fill the gaps in our knowledge as Sir Isaac Newton did when he said: 'I do not know any power in nature which could cause this transverse motion without the divine arm.'[1] The atheist concludes therefore that God has become irrelevant and says that we have no need of that hypothesis. As a result the general public has come to think that science has made belief in a Creator unnecessary and impossible.

1 Turnbull et al., *The Correspondence of Isaac Newton*, 3:240.

A manifest fallacy

But there is a manifest fallacy here. Take a Ford motor car. It is conceivable that a primitive person who was seeing one for the first time and who did not understand the principles of an internal combustion engine, might imagine that there was a god (Mr Ford) inside the engine, making it go. He might further imagine that when the engine ran sweetly, that was because Mr Ford inside the engine liked him, and when it refused to go that was because Mr Ford did not like him. Of course eventually the primitive person would become civilized, learn engineering, and taking the engine to pieces would discover that there was no Mr Ford inside the engine, and that he did not need to introduce Mr Ford as an explanation for the working of the engine. His grasp of the impersonal principles of internal combustion would be altogether enough to explain how the engine worked. So far, so good. But if he then decided that his understanding of the principles of the internal combustion engine made it impossible to believe in the existence of a Mr Ford who designed the engine, this would be patently false. It is likewise a confusion of categories to suppose that our understanding of the impersonal principles according to which the universe works makes it either unnecessary or impossible to believe in the existence of a personal Creator who designed, made and upholds the great engine that is the universe. In other words, we should not confuse the mechanisms by which the universe works with its cause. Every one of us knows how to distinguish between the consciously willed movement of an arm for a purpose and an involuntary spasmodic movement of an arm induced by accidental contact with an electric current.

At this point, however, believers in the myth will tend to reply as follows: 'Well, there might conceivably be a God outside the universe who set it going in the first place. But actually, nothing can be known about him and it is not the task of science to speculate about his possible existence. On the other hand, on the basis of what we now know about the workings of the universe we can confidently assert that even if a God exists outside the universe, he does not, cannot, and never will intervene in its workings. And thus science makes it impossible in particular to believe in the Christian claim that God has invaded nature in the person of Jesus Christ.' Let us now investigate how this part of the myth arises.

The modern myth again

It has been one of the magnificent achievements of science, not only to describe what goes on in the universe, but to discover the invariable laws which govern its workings. It is important here both to understand and to grant what the scientists claim about the nature of these laws. They are not simply descriptions of what happens. They arise from our perception of the essential processes involved. They tell us that, things being as they are, nature not only does work this way, it must work this way and cannot work any other way. The laws not only describe what happened in the past: provided we are not working at the quantum level, they can successfully predict what will happen in the future with such accuracy that, for example, the orbit of the Mir space station can be precisely calculated and Mars landings are possible. It is understandable therefore that many scientists resent the idea that some god could arbitrarily intervene and alter, suspend or reverse the workings of nature. For that would seem to contradict the immutable laws and thus overturn the basis of the scientific understanding of the universe.

But just here there lurks another fallacy which C. S. Lewis illustrated by the following analogy. If this week I put a thousand pounds sterling in the drawer of my desk, add two thousand next week and another thousand the week thereafter, the immutable laws of arithmetic allow me to predict that the next time I come to my drawer, I shall find four thousand pounds. But suppose when I next open the drawer I find only one thousand pounds, what shall I conclude? That the laws of arithmetic have been broken? Certainly not! I might more reasonably conclude that some thief has broken the laws of the State and stolen three thousand pounds out of my drawer. One thing it would be ludicrous to claim is that the laws of arithmetic make it impossible to believe in the existence of such a thief or the possibility of his intervention. On the contrary, it is the normal workings of those laws that have exposed the existence and activity of the thief.

So the laws of nature predict what is bound to happen if God does not intervene; though of course it is no act of thievery if the Creator intervenes in his own creation. To argue that the laws of nature make it impossible for us to believe in the existence of God and the possibility of his intervention in the universe is plainly fallacious. It would be like claiming that an understanding of the laws of the internal combustion engine make it impossible to believe that Mr Ford or one of his mechanics could intervene and remove the cylinder head of a motor car. Of course they could intervene. Moreover this intervention would not destroy those laws. The very same laws that explained why the engine worked with the cylinder head on would now explain why it does not work with the head removed.

In passing we should notice that a belief in God as Creator, far from inhibiting the discovery of nature's laws, has historically been one of the prime motivations in the search for them. Sir Alfred North Whitehead, acknowledged as one of the most eminent historians of science, said: 'Modern science must come from the medieval insistence on the rationality of God.'[2] C. S. Lewis's summary of Whitehead's view is worth mentioning: 'Men became scientific because they expected Law in Nature; and they expected Law in Nature because they believed in a Legislator.'[3] Examples of such men abound: one has only to think of Newton, Kepler, Faraday and Clerk Maxwell. They would all agree with Einstein that science without religion is blind and religion without science is lame.

At this point proponents of the myth may well retort: 'Grant, for the sake of argument, that it is not anti-scientific to concede the theoretical possibility that some god or other may have intervened in our world: what actual evidence is there that any such supernatural event has ever taken place?' Christians will reply, of course, that there is abundant evidence in the miraculous conception, the

2 *Science and the Modern World*, 19.
3 *Miracles*, 110.

miracles and the resurrection of Jesus Christ. To this it will be objected: 'What kind of evidence is this? And how can you expect us to accept it? For after all it comes from the New Testament which was written in a pre-scientific age when people did not understand the laws of nature and for that very reason were all too ready to believe that a miracle had taken place when it hadn't.' Here lies a further fallacy.

A further fallacy

Take for instance the New Testament story that Jesus was born of a virgin without a human father. To say that the early Christians believed this miracle because they did not understand the laws of nature governing the conception and birth of children, is frankly nonsense. They knew all about the fixed laws of nature according to which children are born. If they had not known of those laws they might well have imagined that children could be born without a father or without a mother, but in that case they would not have regarded the story of the birth of Jesus from a virgin as a miracle at all. The very fact that they report it as a miracle shows that they understood perfectly the normal laws governing childbirth. Indeed unless one has first understood that there are laws which normally govern events, how would one ever conclude that a miracle had taken place?

Or take another incident: Luke, who was a doctor trained in the medical science of his day, begins his biography of Christ by raising this very matter (Luke 1:5–25). He tells the story of a man Zechariah and of his wife Elizabeth who for many years had prayed for a son because she was barren. When, in his old age, an angel appeared to him and told him that his former prayers were about to be answered and that his wife would conceive and bear a son, he very politely but firmly refused to believe it. The reason he gave was that he was now old and his wife's body decrepit. For him and his wife to have a child at this stage would run counter to all that he knew of the laws of nature. The interesting thing about him is this: he was no atheist, he was a priest who believed in God and in the existence of angels and the value of prayer. But if the promised fulfilment of his prayer was going to involve a reversal of the laws of nature, he was not prepared to believe it.

The story says that the angel struck him dumb for the sheer illogicality of his unbelief; but it shows this, at least: the early Christians were not a credulous bunch, unaware of the laws of nature and therefore prepared to believe any miraculous story, however absurd. They felt the difficulty in believing the story of such a miracle, just like anyone else. If in the end they believed, it was because they were forced to by the sheer weight of the evidence before their very eyes that a miracle had taken place.

Similarly in his account of the rise of Christianity (the Acts of the Apostles), Luke shows us that the first opposition to the Christian message of the resurrection of Jesus Christ came not from atheists but from the Sadducean high priests in Judaism. They were highly religious men. They believed in God. They said their prayers. But it did not mean that the first time they heard the claim that Jesus had risen from the dead they believed it. They did not believe it, for they had embraced a worldview which did not allow the possibility of such a miracle as the bodily resurrection of Jesus Christ (Acts 23:8).

To suppose then that Christianity was born in a pre-scientific credulous world is simply false to the facts. The ancient world knew as well as we do the law of nature that dead bodies do not get up out of graves. Christianity won its way by dint of the sheer weight of evidence that one man had actually risen from the dead in spite of the laws of nature.

Some people nowadays, it is true, who hold a world-view similar to the ancient Sadducees, have mistakenly tried to make the Christian message more credible to the scientific mind by cutting out the miraculous element altogether from the New Testament and presenting merely the ethical teaching of Jesus. But the device will not work. For, in the first place, the New Testament itself declares that the resurrection of Christ is not some superficial inessential decoration on the Christian message: it constitutes its heart. Excise the heart and you destroy the message. And when the New Testament itself declares this to be the case, it is useless for people two thousand years later to argue that you can cut out the miraculous and still be left with a viable Christianity (1 Cor 15).

In the second place, the whole attempt is misconceived. For our progress in scientific understanding of the laws of nature has made it easier and not more difficult to believe in the resurrection of Christ.

Science on the side of faith

One of the basic laws of nature that science has discovered and constantly promulgates is the Second Law of Thermodynamics which teaches that the universe as a whole is running down, entropy is increasing. But if the universe is running down, it is scarcely possible to think that it has been doing so for an infinitely long time. Indeed science itself teaches that there must have been a point when the reverse process was in operation and the universe was 'wound up'. If then at one point in the past the universe was wound up, it is neither impossible nor unscientific to believe that at the resurrection of Christ the processes of nature once more went into reverse and his dead body came to life and came out of the tomb. Moreover science teaches that while the entropy of the universe considered as a whole is increasing, there can be situations where entropy is decreasing locally. Seeds develop into trees which bring forth fruit; and we know that that is possible because in this local situation the earth is receiving a colossal input of energy from the sun. Consistent with this, the New Testament points out that the resurrection of Christ was made possible by an unimaginably great input of energy from the Creator himself: 'the immeasurable greatness of his power ... the working of his great might that he worked in Christ when he raised him from the dead' (Eph 1:19–20).

Notwithstanding this, some people may feel a continuing difficulty which they will express as follows: 'This evidence in the New Testament is now for us very remote. How can we possibly have any direct access to it? After all, miracles in general and the resurrection of Christ in particular are not things that happen every day of the week or every week of the year. We have no modern experience to act as a basis of comparison and as a criterion by means of which to measure their credibility. Are we then simply expected to believe everything the New Testament writers say just because they say it?'

The nature of Christ's miracles

The answer is that there are many considerations which we can bring to bear on the record of these miracles for the purpose of assessing their credibility. To begin with, we can notice the difference between the miracles which the New Testament says Jesus did and the silly miracle stories invented by credulous people in later degenerate centuries of Christendom. In these later stories stone images weep tears of blood, wolves turn into humans and birds spring out of lumps of clay. There is nothing remotely like this in the miracle stories in the New Testament. The miracles of Christ were congruent with the normal workings of nature. When Jesus miraculously produced wine he did not conjure it out of the air: he called for water and turned that water into wine. That is what nature does every year by using intervening means of a vine and soil, sun and rain. Had Christ incongruously produced wine from thin air we might have supposed that here was some alien magical power with no respect for nature and her laws. Christ's miracles show a respect for nature as one might expect from the Creator of nature. At the same time they show him, understandably, superior to nature.

We may also consider the moral quality of his miracles. None was ever done to harm anyone, not even to destroy his enemies.

Instructive too are the terms which the New Testament uses for the miracles of Jesus. Sometimes they are called by a word which denotes an act of power. On other occasions they are referred to by a word which means a wonder, or portent. Together these words indicate that Christ deliberately performed acts of supernatural power in order forcefully to focus attention on himself. But beyond this they were intended to function as signs pointing to those great spiritual resources that Christ can make available to all people of all times and places.

This is an aspect of Christ's miracles that is particularly emphasized by the writer of the Fourth Gospel whose normal word for miracle is 'sign' (though this is unfortunately obscured in many translations by the use of the word 'miracle' instead of 'sign'). So, for instance, John tells us that when Christ miraculously multiplied the loaves of bread, he did it, not merely to feed the people's stomachs, but to call attention to the fact that he is himself the Bread of Life that can satisfy the spiritual hunger of men and women of all ages, who by faith believe him and receive him as Saviour and Lord (John 6). And at this level it is open to every one of us to prove in our personal experience whether this is true or not.

An experiment

And the ultimate verification is this. If Christ did, in fact, rise from the dead on the third day—and he did—that means he is alive today and ready by his Spirit to enter into a personal relationship with us if we on our side are prepared to enter into a personal relationship with him. Like any relationship, you cannot experience and prove its reality unless you are prepared to enter into it. But the possibility of entering in is open to us all. That is what John means when he says of the miracles of Jesus: 'these are written so that you may believe that Jesus is the Christ, the Son of God, and that by believing you may have life in his name' (John 20:31).

Here then is an experiment that any and every one can make. If Jesus is indeed God's Son, the Gospel of John comes to us with his authority. It is God's way of getting in touch with us. Millions have testified that through their reading of it God made himself known to them personally. We cannot write off all those millions as fools. The only truly scientific thing to do is to put the claim to the test by making the experiment and reading the Gospel ourselves.

CHAPTER 4

But don't all religions lead to God?

It surely is no exaggeration to say that for many people nowadays atheism is scarcely any longer a viable creed. The difficulty that keeps people from abandoning it altogether, however, is their uncertainty as to what creed they could satisfactorily put in its place. It is not self-evident to them that the obvious alternative to atheism is Christianity. Granted that the only alternative to atheism is to believe in a god of some sort: but why, they ask themselves, must that be the God of Christianity? Why not Shiva, Vishnu, Rama, Krishna or any one or all of the multitudinous gods of Hinduism? Or Allah, the one and only God of Islam? Or could indeed Theravada Buddhism be the most attractive alternative to atheism? Unlike Mahayana Buddhism, which believes in ten thousand and one deities, Theravada Buddhism is not, strictly speaking, a religion at all, but a philosophy which does not believe in any god whatever. Nonetheless it offers its adherents a body of doctrine (the

Three Pitakas) and a set of disciplines calculated to deliver them from the tyranny of their desires and to lead them into a way of life increasingly free from turmoil, stress, and fear and into peaceful relations with their fellow men and women.

Then again, the purpose of all religion, so many people feel, is to produce acceptable behaviour. What therefore does it matter, they say, which particular system you choose, so long as you follow the precepts of your chosen religion consistently and sincerely? If the moral goal is the same, what does it matter from what direction and by what path one climbs the mountain? You get to the same summit in the end. Do not all the spokes of a wheel lead to the hub? As George Bernard Shaw put it: 'There is only one religion in the world, though there are a hundred versions of it.'[1] Do not, then, all religions lead to God?

What religions say about themselves

However, not all the individual religions will agree that they are simply alternative routes to the same goal. The Buddha claimed that, 'there is one sole way for the purification of human beings'[2] and that, 'truth is one, there is not a second.'[3] Monotheistic Judaism will never agree with Hinduism that there are millions of gods. And Christianity will say to monotheistic Judaism and Islam that there is no name under heaven given amongst men other than the

1 *Plays Pleasant and Unpleasant*, Vol. II, preface (1898) from *Oxford Essential Quotations*.
2 Zaehner, *The Concise Encyclopaedia of Living Faiths*, 265.
3 Zaehner, 275.

name of Jesus by which we must be saved (Acts 4:12). To many people these mutually exclusive claims to uniqueness seem arrogant and dangerously out of place in the global village which the world has become. Would it not then be best for an ex-atheist to follow the eclectic philosophy of the New Age Movement, taking what he likes out of all religions, and combining elements of animism, nature worship, pantheism and Christian morality into one pragmatic amalgam? New Age, denying the objective existence of truth, can accommodate almost any religious belief—provided that belief makes no absolute claims for itself.

Cogent as all this may seem, however, we must be on our guard lest its very attractiveness is an illusion unsupported by the facts.

Take first the contention that it does not matter which system a person follows provided that person is sincere. In no other department of life would any responsible person be content to take sincerity as a guarantee of either truth or safety. All forms of medical practice have by definition the same goal, namely the healing of the sick. But not all medicines are equally potent or equally safe. Some medicines have ruinous side effects. Some are poison. We would not be wise to swallow the contents of a bottle indiscriminately simply because the label bore the word 'medicine'. We all believe in the objectivity of truth where medicine is concerned!

Secondly, even if it were true—and it is not—that the chief aim of all religions is to get people to behave well towards one another, it would not be safe to suppose without further investigation that behaving well towards one another is a sufficient goal to aim at. In centuries gone by, the seas of the world were sailed by many pirate ships. In some of those ships the pirates doubtless behaved very well towards one another and had rigorous and well-kept rules to ensure that the booty they captured was fairly shared out. In that sense they may well have been satisfied with the standard of morality they had achieved. But that would have overlooked the fundamental fact that they were pirates in rebellion against the lawful government on land! If that government had caught them, their morality would not have saved them from hanging. To suppose that the chief aim of religion is to get us to behave well towards one another overlooks the question as to whether there is a supreme being, a Creator who made us, to whom we owe allegiance and who will call us to account for our disloyalty and neglect of him. If there is such a supreme being and we have ignored him and broken his laws, it will be no excuse when he calls us to account, to plead that we have behaved well towards our fellow human beings. And here there is an unbridgeable chasm between, say, Theravada Buddhism on the one hand and Christianity on the other. To the Theravada Buddhists, man in his eternal essence, is the greatest spiritual presence in the universe.[4] In Judaism and Christianity, for a man to adopt that attitude about himself is tantamount to blasphemy. For them, man is certainly made in the image of God; but man is not God. God remains the greatest spiritual reality; and for man to usurp his place is the height of rebellion against the Most High.

Moreover there is another irreconcilable difference between religions like Hinduism and Buddhism on the one

4 Zaehner, 409.

hand and Judaism and Christianity on the other. The former pair maintain that the material world is an illusion (*maya*) and that the wise man's true goal is to escape from the material world into an immaterial nirvana. Judaism and Christianity flatly deny that. They affirm that the material creation as it left the Creator's hand was good, that our material bodies were likewise good; and though spoiled by sin, they will one day be physically resurrected. Here then are two irreconcilably opposed worldviews. It would be a sign of very shallow thinking to suppose that one could take the best out of them both and put it together. And it will obviously make an enormous difference to a man's attitude to the world around him and even to his own body, which of the two views he adopts.

Religions and the problem of guilt

It is true of course that when it comes to the basic precepts of morality—honouring one's parents, doing no murder, etc.—all religions teach more or less the same. Compare, for example, the Five Precepts of Buddhism with the Ten Commandments of Judaism. In a word, religions teach us that we ought to be good. But our trouble is that we have not been good. We have sinned against God, broken his laws, and incurred their penalties. We have sinned against our fellow men and women and done them damage. We have sinned against ourselves; and if we are indeed God's creatures, then to sin against our fellow men and against ourselves is also a grievous sin against God. Human beings are so made that when they have sinned against God and their fellow men, they develop a guilty conscience which wrecks their peace of mind and haunts them like a skeleton in the cupboard. To enter into peace, to face the future with confidence, they must be able to get rid of that guilty conscience. Thus any religion worthy of the name must deal with this question of guilt. But how? It is worse than useless to attempt to get rid of guilt from the conscience by telling men and women that their past sin and guilt do not matter. For in the end that would mean that the people against whom they have sinned do not matter, the damage they have done does not matter, and that conscience is a mere weakness of character that can conveniently be suppressed with impunity. No paradise could ever be built on a theory like this which implies that in the end human beings do not matter; though, sadly, the attempt has been made more than once.

Every man and woman urgently needs therefore a solution to this problem that can uphold their moral standards and their sense of justice and at the same time bring them forgiveness and set them justly free from the chains of past guilt.

Here of course the great religions differ and it is no use hiding the fact. Certain forms of Buddhism deny that there is any such thing as forgiveness. Men and women simply have to suffer their inevitable karma of demerit which each individual accumulates for himself throughout his present and past lives, until it is exhausted and they are released into their hoped-for nirvana. They can expect no outside help. 'No one can purify another.'[5] There is only the inexorable operation of the law of cause and effect,

5 Zaehner, 265

and any excess of demerit over merit must be worked off in a possibly endless succession of reincarnations.

Some early forms of Hinduism did suggest that forgiveness could be obtained by the offering of ceremonial gifts and sacrifices to the gods. Judaism likewise had an elaborate system of sacrifices on the grounds of which people could find forgiveness from God. But Judaism itself was careful to point out that the sacrificing of bullocks and cows could not possibly be regarded as an adequate solution to the problem of human guilt (Ps 40:6). After all, what do cows know about sin? They do not go to bed at night haunted by a guilty conscience. Moral considerations remain forever above their heads. It is the glory and burden of human beings to be conscious of the demands of morality.

At best, therefore, animal sacrifices were but a symbolic way of acknowledging that the penalty of sin must be paid if conscience is to have rest through forgiveness. Nowadays Judaism has lost even that system of symbols and has nothing to put in its place. In this it resembles Islam that teaches people to cast themselves on the mercy of the Almighty, but cannot point to any sacrifice that can adequately pay the price of sin.

Christ's unquestionable uniqueness

In this connection Christianity is unique. For although it teaches people to be good, that is not the major thrust of its message. The heart of its message is that God the judge, against whom we have all sinned, has taken upon himself the task of upholding the honour of his law and of public justice by providing his Son as a sacrifice to take away the sin of the world. In this Christ is unique. Of all the great founders and leaders of religions he is the only one who will come alongside us claiming to be our Creator incarnate, come to deal with the problem of the guilt of our sin by means of his sacrifice at Calvary so that we may receive forgiveness and peace with God. For example, as H. D. Lewis asserts: '. . . and Buddha himself, according to the famous text which describes his disease, disavowed at the time of his death any peculiar claims to be made on his behalf as the instrument of salvation.'[6] To ask why we must think that Christ is the only way to God is to miss the point completely. No one else offers to deal with this fundamental problem. Christ is the only one in the running. It is not narrow-mindedness to accept from Christ what nobody else offers!

It is moreover important to be clear about the basic condition on which Christ's offer is made, for here once more is an area in which Christianity is unique.

Since not all of those who profess Christianity have seen this distinction, we underline it by considering the familiar metaphor which represents religion as a way or a path. In Buddhism it is the 'Eightfold Path', or 'Middle Way'; and from very early times Christianity was known as 'The Way'. In this scheme of things there is usually a gateway at the beginning through which one must enter, some ritual or experience through which one must pass in order to set out on the way. In many there is also a gate at the end that leads to heaven or nirvana, etc.—although

6 *The Study of Religions*, 168.

the Zen Buddhists claim that enlightenment (*satori*) is possible in this present life. The idea common to them all is that whether you get through the final gate or not (or, achieve enlightenment along the Path or not) all depends on how you progress along the way—the basic principle is merit. People often think of it in the same way as they do of a university degree. If you wish to gain a degree from a university, you must pass through the necessary entrance examination in order to qualify to enter the university. Unless you pass through that gate, you cannot even begin the university course that you hope will lead to a degree. But entering through that gate at the beginning is no guarantee that you will get a degree at the end of the course. For there is another gate at the end of the course, namely the final examination. Whether you will ever get through that gate will depend on how well you have performed both in the course and in the final examination. The professors will do their best to help you, but even they cannot guarantee that you will pass. In the end it all depends on your merit. You have to earn the degree, and whether you have done enough to earn it cannot be decided until the final examination.

In the popular mind Christianity itself is a religion of this kind. In order to gain salvation and acceptance with God you must first enter through the gate at the beginning of the road, namely the ritual of baptism. Entering that gate puts you in the running for salvation; but of course it doesn't mean that you are already saved. Whether you ever achieve salvation and acceptance with God depends on passing the examination at the end of the course, namely the final judgment; and passing that final judgment must depend on the progress you have made and the merit you have attained during life. Of course the church and its officers are there to help you all they can; but even they cannot guarantee that you will pass the final judgment. Thus the question whether you will in the end be accepted by God must be left open until the final assessment, for the very good reason that acceptance with God is thought to depend upon one's works, progress and merit.

Now this, however plausible it sounds, is the very opposite of what the New Testament actually teaches about acceptance with God, for in this matter Christianity goes clean counter to all religion. It says quite categorically that salvation is not by works and merit. It is the gift of God (Eph 2:8–9). As a free gift, therefore, it cannot be made to depend on how well one has progressed on the path. The question then arises: At what point along the way does one receive this gift? At what point does God give us the assurance that he has accepted us? At the end of the way? No! At the very beginning of the way, as the Lord Jesus explained to his contemporaries: 'Truly, truly, I say to you, whoever hears my word and believes him who sent me has eternal life. He does not come into judgment, but *has passed* from death to life' (John 5:24). Or, as Paul put it: 'Therefore, since we *have been justified* by faith, we have peace with God through our Lord Jesus Christ. Through him we have also obtained access by faith into this grace in which we stand, and we rejoice in hope of the glory of God' (Rom 5:1–2). What is more, we see in both these statements the assurance that, on the ground of having been justified at the beginning of the road, God assures us that we shall pass the gate at the end of the road as well. As the Apostle Paul puts it: 'Since, therefore, we have now been justified by his blood, much more shall we be saved by him from the wrath of God' (Rom 5:9).

Too good to be true?

At first sight this seems so contrary to what most people have ever thought, that they are inclined to dismiss it out of hand and to consider that it cannot be a true interpretation of Christianity. And yet this basic security and sense of acceptance with God was central in the teaching of Jesus:

> My sheep hear my voice, and I know them, and they
> follow me. I give them eternal life, and they will never
> perish, and no one will snatch them out of my hand.
> My Father, who has given them to me, is greater
> than all, and no one is able to snatch them out of the
> Father's hand. (John 10:27–29)

But, in case we still find it hard to accept that a believer in Christ can enjoy in this life the peace of complete acceptance with God, let us consider, by way of analogy the deepest of human relationships, that between a man and his wife. In order to ensure a happy marriage would it be wise of a husband to leave it as long as possible after a wedding before allowing his wife to know that he has accepted her? We have only to ask the question to answer it. For a woman to spend the whole of her married life uncertain whether she had done enough to gain acceptance with her husband would transform her married life into a kind of slavery. In normal marriages the husband assures his wife of his acceptance of her and of his lifelong commitment to her from the very beginning. It is the wife's confidence in her husband's love and acceptance of her from the very start that brings out her devotion to him and his to her.

The analogy is not far-fetched. According to Christianity, salvation is not a scheme for piling up merit that buys acceptance with God. It is a question of entering into a present personal relationship with our Creator which the Bible describes in terms of a husband's love for his wife (Eph 5:22–33). That relationship is not to be left uncertain until the end of life. Indeed, if ever it is to be formed, it must be formed now in this life. But once it is formed it will last eternally.

Yet again, it seems to many people that this simply cannot be true; for if it were, it would, they think, be positively dangerous. 'If we could be sure in this life of acceptance with God,' they say, 'would it not lead us to abuse his love and his grace by unworthy living?'

The question seems reasonable enough, particularly to people who have never experienced what happens when one responds to Christ's invitation, and enters into this personal relationship with Him. But the answer to the question is No, decidedly, No. And it is No, because of the nature of the gate through which we must enter in order to begin the Christian pathway. The gate is not the rite of infant baptism performed on a baby who is quite unaware of what is happening. It is genuine new birth produced in a person by the regenerating power of the

Holy Spirit (Titus 3:3–7; John 3:5–16). It is not achieved by a person's effort and works; it is a gift given to everyone who personally repents and personally receives Christ as Lord and Saviour (John 1:12–13; Eph 2:8–10). But because the gift is the gift of new spiritual life, with new powers, new desires, new goals, and above all a new relationship with God, it naturally leads to good works, indeed to a whole new lifestyle. This does not mean that the believer is sinlessly perfect, but when he sins a true believer will repent and confess his sins and receive God's promised forgiveness (1 John 1:9).

This then is the glory of the Christian gospel. But it carries a serious corollary. When there is no evidence of a changed lifestyle, there is every reason to doubt whether this new birth has ever taken place, whether indeed the person concerned has ever personally entered the gate. Scripture says 'As the body apart from the spirit is dead, so also faith apart from works is dead' (Jas 2:26). A baby does not get life by crying; but a new-born baby that doesn't cry, is probably stillborn.

Christ's truth claim is not tyrannous

A final point arises in connection with Christ's claim to be the unique Saviour. For example, he said 'I am the way, and the truth, and the life. No one comes to the Father except through me' (John 14:6). Similarly his apostles proclaimed his uniqueness: 'There is salvation in no one else, for there is no other name under heaven given among men by which we must be saved' (Acts 4:12). Now in an increasingly pluralistic world, many people are very uneasy when they hear such claims. They share the fear articulated by Karl Popper in his famous book, *The Open Society*, that the belief that one has the truth is always implicitly totalitarian. Popper points out that it is just a short step from the confidence which says, 'I am sure . . .' to the tyranny which says, '. . . therefore I must be obeyed'. This leads Popper to the view that all absolute truth claims must be rejected to safeguard society.[7] Since history provides us with too many examples of the realization of this fear, it is vitally important that we see that Christ who did make such claims, repudiated violence and tyranny. Indeed this is one of the glories of the Christian message that Christ did not force his way into people's lives by demonstrations of naked power—and he did not lack power. He wanted men and women to come to trust and love God—and trust and love cannot be compelled, they can only be won. Christ rather demonstrated his love and care for people, as the Gospels describe in great detail. And when some people nevertheless rejected him and asked him to leave, he did not violently force them to submit to him but rather accepted their verdict and sadly went away (Matt 8:34-9:1). When his disciples took swords in order to defend him, he stopped them at once by uttering the famous words: 'Put your sword back into its place. For all who take the sword will perish by the sword' (Matt 26:52). To the Roman Procurator Pilate, before whom he had been arraigned as a potential insurrectionist leader, he said: 'My kingdom is not of this world. If my kingdom were of this world, my servants would have been fighting, that I might not be delivered over to the

7 See *The Open Society*.

Jews . . .' (John 18:36). Responding to this statement, with the full authority of Rome behind him, Pilate pronounced: 'I find no guilt in him' (John 18:38). The context is Christ's statement to Pilate that he was a king come into the world 'to bear witness to the truth. Everyone who is of the truth listens to my voice' (John 18:37). Thus Pilate's verdict shows that he saw no political threat in Christ's claim. Moreover, Christ even prayed for the soldiers who were detailed to crucify him. He cannot, therefore be held responsible for those of his professed followers who, in direct disobedience to his explicit command, have used force and violence to tyrannize others. Such behaviour is simply not Christian, whatever it may maintain to the contrary. Christ's claims, if genuinely accepted, lead people to obey his teaching and, in particular, to love even their enemies. Christ cannot fairly be criticized for the behaviour of those who all down the centuries and still to this day reject his teaching and turn Christianity into a tyranny.

CHAPTER 5

But if there is a God, why do so many people suffer?

Providing satisfying answers to this problem is necessarily a complicated task. When people are comparatively free of suffering themselves, and can take an objective and dispassionate view of the matter, they look for rational explanations that can satisfy their intellects. On the other hand, when people have suffered, or are still suffering, mental and physical anguish, or are smarting under a sense of massive injustice, mere rational explanations are scarcely enough. They look for answers that will satisfy not only their heads, but their hearts; answers that will soothe their anguish, strengthen their faith, give them hope, strength and courage to endure.

Let me illustrate the point. Suppose you are the parents of a twelve-year-old girl, and it is discovered that she has a defective spine. The doctors say that she needs a long series of complicated bone transplant operations to build up and reinforce her vertebrae. If she does not begin to have these operations now, it will be too late when she is older, and in later life she will develop very bad and painful curvature of the spine. The question is: Shall she have the operations or not? The girl cannot be left to take the decision by herself: she is too young to understand and envisage all the issues involved. You, the parents will, in the end, have to take the decision for her. What will you tell her?

You will doubtless begin by explaining in terms she can understand the physiological reasons why the operations are necessary, and why there is no other way of making her better. You will tell her honestly that it will involve pain, but that the surgeons are very kind and very clever and that in the end the outcome will be so good that she will be glad she had the operations. In other words, you will feel it very important to prepare her intellectually to face the ordeal.

The trouble is, however, that at the moment she is not in any great pain; but, if she takes the treatment, every time she wakes up from the long drawn out series of operations to which you have committed her, and for months thereafter, she will be in excruciating pain. How will you respond when she then sobs, 'Why did you let me in for this terrible pain?' Mere intellectual explanations will hardly be enough. You will now need to assure her of your love, to let her feel that you are with her in her suffering, and to build up her hope that it is going to be all right in the end. And meanwhile you will do all you can to strengthen her faith in you, in your love, in your wisdom and in the doctors; for if she loses that faith, her battle against pain will be immensely harder and could even be lost.

So it is with us adults when we face first the intellectual problem of suffering, and then the experience of suffering itself. We shall need more than one kind of answer. Let us start, however, with the intellectual problem.

The intellectual problem

It is, actually, a two-fold problem, because suffering comes upon us from two logically distinct sources (though in practice the two sources are sometimes inextricably intertwined). One source is the evil for which man is himself directly responsible, i.e. commercial, political and civil injustice, exploitation, aggression, torture, murder, rape, child abuse, adultery, treachery, slavery, genocide, wars, and such like things, and, in addition, all those wrongs, minor in scale maybe, which nonetheless account perhaps for the most widespread misery in our world, namely the hurtful, damaging things that we all do to one another. By convention we call this the problem of evil.

The other source of suffering is natural disasters: earthquakes, volcanoes, tidal waves, floods, landslides, avalanches, ultra-violet rays, droughts, blights, famines, plagues (e.g. locusts or malarial mosquitoes), for which man is not immediately responsible (though he may contribute indirectly to some of them by irresponsibly damaging the ecosystem) and other things like congenital deformities and personality-destroying diseases, for which again man is not immediately responsible (though he may contribute to some of them both directly and indirectly). By convention we call this the problem of pain.

Whether from the one source or the other, suffering strongly challenges faith in God. The problem of pain says: 'How can we believe that a world in which there are so many natural disasters has been created by an all-loving, all-powerful and all-wise, personal, God?' The problem of evil adds: 'How can we reconcile the existence of enormous evil, and the fact that it is allowed to continue, with the existence of an all-powerful, all-holy, God who is supposed to be concerned for justice?' The intellectual problem, then, is certainly severe: it would be foolish to deny it, or even to underestimate it.

A solution that makes matters worse

Actually, however, there is one simple way of eliminating this intellectual problem forthwith: embrace atheism! Deny there is a God. Then there is no problem at all in accounting for evil and pain. For if there is no intelligent Creator, we must suppose that our world, and we ourselves within it, were brought into being by mindless, impersonal, forces, which unconsciously produced and developed mindless matter. Then after millions of years of random permutations, this mindless matter gave rise to intelligent minds which could protest against suffering. But it did so accidentally. It had no intention of doing it; and having done it, it did not realize what it had done. It simply continued to proceed in its thoughtless, unplanned way, without any ultimate goal in sight, untroubled by whether the result was good or bad, intellectually acceptable or otherwise. On this supposition, then, there would be no difficulty at all in accounting for the existence of evil and pain. What else could be expected from this mindless procedure but a colossal amount of pain at every turn? (There would now, of course, be an insurmountable difficulty in accounting for the detailed, sophisticated design and the great beauty which we observe everywhere in the universe.)

Atheism, then, undeniably gets rid of the intellectual problem of suffering: *but it does not get rid of the pain*, nor help us to bear it. In fact, it can make the pain harder to bear. For if there is a personal God and he created us, then there is solid ground for believing that suffering is not simply destructive and ultimately meaningless but can be used by God for our eternal good. And the reasoning behind this deduction is simple enough. Normal human parents accept moral responsibility for the children whom they have brought into the world, love them and seek their good. Such parents, moreover, find this concern for their children in-built in their very nature. It is highly unlikely, then, that the God who created them and placed this concern in their hearts, is himself utterly unconcerned for his creatures and accepts no moral responsibility for having created them (Luke 11:13). Here then is solid ground for hope; and when people are in the midst of suffering pain or injustice, such hope is often the one thing that can comfort, support and help them to endure. It is in contexts like this that the Bible comments:

> And not only the creation, but we ourselves, who have the firstfruits of the Spirit, groan inwardly as we wait eagerly for adoption as sons, the redemption of our bodies. For in this hope we were saved. Now hope that

is seen is not hope. For who hopes for what he sees?
But if we hope for what we do not see, we wait for it
with patience. (Rom 8:23–25)

But atheism removes such hope altogether. It leaves
people in their pain, injury and grief, without comfort,
either emotional or spiritual, while their intellects have to
submit to the tyrannous irrationality of pointless, hopeless
suffering brought on them by mindless, heartless, forces
which are unfortunately their masters.

Take a young mother of thirty-three years, whose husband has just been shot by criminals, and she herself has
been diagnosed as having terminal cancer. What can an
atheist say to her? Her sense of justice has been outraged
by her husband's murder. But the atheist, if he is honest,
will have to say that her sense of justice is no guarantee
that there is any objective justice in the world or in the
universe. Her husband did not get justice in this life; and
he will get no justice in the life to come either, for there
is no life to come, nor any God to see that ultimately
justice shall be done. Hope of justice has proved for him
an empty dream. And as for her, the atheist will have to
say that there was never any ultimate purpose behind
her existence anyway; nor is there any goal beyond her
very short life for her to look forward to; her suffering
and pain are utterly valueless. There is, therefore, no hope.
Atheists are, as the Bible puts it, 'Separated from Christ, . . .
having no hope and without God in the world' (Eph 2:12).

Atheism's solution to the problem of evil and pain thus
adds to the pain. Emotionally, morally, and intellectually it
is simply destructive.

There are other attempts to solve the problem which fall short of atheism—but which also fall short of the picture of God which we get in the Bible. The most common of them is that of admitting that God is all-good, but denying that he is all-powerful. However this 'solution' is no real solution at all because once more it solves the intellectual problem to some extent but totally fails in the same way as atheism does to provide someone who is capable of helping us face our suffering.

This leads us then to a key question: is there any ground at all for thinking that suffering, from whatever source, is not incompatible with the existence of an all-loving, all-powerful, and all-wise Creator, who in spite of the suffering he allows, is loyal to us his creatures, has a glorious destiny for us, if we will have it, and can use the pain the better to prepare us for that destiny?

An answer to the problem of evil

Let us begin with the problem of evil, since the evil perpetrated by man on man is actually responsible for vastly more suffering than natural disasters are. Take the twentieth century and up to the present. The millions that have perished in natural disasters have been few compared with the billions slaughtered by two world wars, and countless other wars; by right-wing and left-wing dictators, by Hitler and Stalin, Pol Pot and warlords in the DR Congo and other countries in Africa; by religious and political persecution; by Mafia and terrorist organizations; by the sophisticated violence of Hiroshima and Nagasaki, and by the sub-human savagery of Yugoslavia and Rwanda; by democratic nations who boost their economies by manufacturing arms and selling them to repressive governments who have no respect for human rights; by industrialists who make fortunes by manufacturing millions of landmines which they then sell to Afghanistan and Angola where they will blow the legs off thousands of innocent civilians including children; by the exploitation of poorer countries by richer countries and by corruption in poor countries which puts millions of dollars of international aid into the pockets of their dictators while they leave their own people in squalor and poverty. Compared with all this deliberate evil, a natural disaster like a volcano seems innocent.

The understandable reaction of many people to this unending flood of evil is to say, 'Is not God supposed to be concerned for justice? And is he not supposed to be almighty? Why then, if there is a God, does he not put a stop to all this evil?'

Well, the Bible says that he will most certainly put an end to it one day. God 'has fixed a day on which he will judge the world in righteousness by a man whom he has appointed; and of this he has given assurance to all by raising him from the dead' (Acts 17:31).

'But what use to us', many people say, 'is the promise that one day in the distant future, at the end of the world, God will put a stop to all evil? Why, if God really exists, does he not do it now by intervening and destroying, or somehow putting out of action, all bad and evil men? He is supposed to be Almighty, isn't he? He could do it. Why doesn't he?'

Well, he certainly could do it, and in some extreme cases he does. The Bible records that at one stage in history God blotted out the whole human race (except eight people) by a gigantic flood (Gen 6–8), as he will eventually do again, only this time not by water but by what sounds from the description of it (2 Pet 3) like atomic fusion.[1] Similarly, when the extreme immorality of Sodom and Gomorrah became intolerable, God judged these cities by incinerating them (Gen 19).

The problem with indiscriminate judgment

But there is a problem, which the Bible itself explicitly mentions in connection with Sodom and Gomorrah. When gross sin and evil infect a whole society, how can a righteous God destroy the comparatively innocent along with the extremely guilty? With a small city like Sodom it was moderately easy to arrange for the few comparatively innocent people to escape the general destruction. But sometimes gross evil infects whole nations, countries, empires; and then millions of people get caught up to differing degrees in the cruel and arrogant policies of their rulers. School teachers are obliged to inject the minds of their pupils with, say, rabid fascism and genocidal hatred of minorities (as in Hitler's Germany), or with God-defying atheism (as in Marxist countries). Men are forced, by a false patriotism, to engage in cruel ideological wars of imperial expansion. University professors are pressurized into reinterpreting history (and sometimes even science) in accordance with government policy regardless of what

1 Sceptics often deride such biblical statements; and yet they will then turn round and point to evidence that at one stage in history almost all life on this planet was in fact extinguished.

they know to be the truth. And in that case how could a righteous God destroy whole nations without simultaneously destroying masses of comparatively innocent (though still sinful) people along with the guilty?

'But that's just the point', says someone. 'If God is all-wise as well as all-powerful, he could conduct a selective judgment of everybody individually, eliminate the bad, and leave the good. Then why doesn't he?'

Well, suppose he did. Suppose he intervened today and destroyed all bad and sinful individuals everywhere throughout the world without exception. Where in fairness would he stop? And how many would be left? Where would he draw the line between the bad and the good? And who are the bad people anyway, and who are the good? 'Get rid of the capitalists', say the communists 'and you will have a good world of good people.' The capitalists, of course, say the opposite. And bringing it down to the personal level, what would God have to say to each one of us?

And there are other considerations. Let's imagine two men who are selfish, cruel, given to bad temper and violence, to lies and treachery. One man is a private citizen and has little power; but his evil behaviour blights his wife's life, breaks up their marriage and does his children serious, if not irreparable, psychological damage. The other man is the dictator of his country. He has immense power, and because of it his evil behaviour leads to the suffering and death of thousands. What would the first man have done, if he had had the same power as the second? Which, therefore, is at heart the worse man?

According to the Bible, God's verdict on us as individuals is in fact that we have all sinned, I, you and everyone else. Judged by God's absolute standards we are all bad; not all to the same degree, but all to some degree. None of us is guiltless (Rom 3:10–20, 23).

But God is not only just, he is compassionate and merciful. The people of the ancient city of Nineveh, and especially their rulers, were notoriously cruel, and to strengthen their imperialist power engaged in mass deportation of the populations whom they conquered. God threatened them with destruction because of it, but he was prepared to delay the execution of his judgment in order to give them opportunity to repent; and he rebuked the Israelite prophet, Jonah, for demanding their immediate destruction (Jon 1:1–2; 3:1–4:11).

On similar grounds the New Testament explains why God is prepared to wait what for us is a long time before he brings the world to an end and puts a complete stop to evil: 'The Lord is not slow to fulfil his promise as some count slowness, but is patient toward you, not wishing that any should perish, but that all should reach repentance. But the day of the Lord [= Day of Judgment] will come . . .' (2 Pet 3:9–10).

'But if God is going to accuse us all of being bad and sinners,' says someone, 'he is supposed to have created us, isn't he? Then why did he not create us in such a way as we could not sin and do evil?'

The glory and inevitable cost of being human

Well, he could have done; but that would have meant denying us any kind of free will and genuinely free choice. In that case we should have been, not morally responsible human beings, but more like preprogrammed humanoid robots. And I don't know any human being who would prefer to be a robot.

To be a genuinely moral being you have to be able to understand the difference between good and evil, and then to be able to choose freely either to do good or to do evil. A computer can have an enormous amount of 'knowledge' stored within it, but it has no understanding of what it 'knows', nor any moral choice. A computer can only choose to do what it is programmed to do. If it makes the wrong choice, or breaks down, it cannot be blamed for it. It has no responsibility for it. It feels no guilt. It does not understand what guilt is, or what it feels like to be guilty. It cannot even tell you what it feels like to be a computer, let alone a guilty computer (or a happy computer for that matter). Human beings, as we can all observe, are not in that sense programmed by their Creator. They have the ability to choose and generally pride themselves on it. When a man has chosen, for instance, to face danger rather than take the cowardly way out, he likes to be regarded as having been responsible for the choice and to be praised for it. Most people would feel it an insult to be treated as a baby, or as mentally incompetent or as a machine that was not responsible for its actions. It is only when we have done something very wrong that we are tempted to deny responsibility and to say, 'I couldn't help it.'

God, then, could certainly have made us like robots; but in that case, again, we should have been incapable of true, mature love freely given and received. If you were sitting in your room and a robot entered, flung its arms round your neck and said, 'I love you', you would either laugh at the absurdity of it, or else push it away in disgust, or both. A robot has no concept of love in the first place; and even if it had, it would not be free to decide by itself either to love you or not to love you: it could only do what it was programmed by somebody else to do. It has no independent personality.

Here then is the glory of being human. God has created man as a moral being, able to perceive the beauty of his Creator's holiness and the moral splendour of his character. God has also endowed him with free will and the ability to love so that he can freely choose to love, trust, worship and obey his Creator, and enjoy true friendship and fellowship with God both here on earth and eventually in God's heaven (John 4:22–24).

But, of course, the choice God gave man was not, and could not be, a choice between two equally good alternatives. God is the totality of good, and there can be no permanent good apart from him. To say No to God, the source of life, is by definition to say Yes to ultimate disaster and death. There are not, and cannot be, two paradises, one with the Creator, and one without him. From the very beginning, therefore, God warned man of the fatal consequences that would inevitably follow if man chose to disbelieve and disobey God and to go his own way. The Bible says, however, that the first man, Adam, did precisely that: he chose to disobey God, to go his own way, to take what he felt was a better course (Gen 2, 3; Rom 5:12). And we all have to a greater or lesser extent done the same thing (Isa 53:6; Rom 3:23), with the evil results that we see everywhere around us, and within us, today. Thus, according to the Bible, evil is evil because it is rebellion against God. But whose fault is that?

But once more someone objects: 'Is not God supposed to be omniscient and able to foresee all possible eventualities?'

Yes, of course.

'Then did he not foresee that if he gave man free will, man would abuse it, choose evil, and bring disaster on himself and the whole world?'

Yes, God did foresee it.

'Then how could God possibly justify going ahead and giving man free will in the first place?'

God's safety net

Because even before he created mankind he had decided to provide a safety net, available to all, so that in spite of their rebellion, waywardness, sin and evil, none of them need perish permanently. He would, in fact, take the occasion of man's sin to demonstrate, not merely in words, but in action, that with a Creator's heart he loved all his creatures even while they were still sinners. He puts it this way in the Bible:

> For one will scarcely die for a righteous person—though
> perhaps for a good person one would dare even to die—
> but God shows his love for us in that while we were
> still sinners, Christ died for us. (Rom 5:7–8)

A way was to be made for man, when he discovered the ruinous results of sin, to repent, to come back to God and be forgiven, to be reconciled and restored into fellowship with him. God himself, through his Son, Jesus Christ, would pay the penalty of man's sin for, and on behalf of, man. And the cost of all the reparations made necessary by the damage caused by man's sin, which man's own resources could never pay, would be borne by God. What is more, the guarantee would also be given that when the final day of judgment comes and God rises up to punish the unrepentant and to put an end to evil for ever, then those who have repented and put their faith in God and his Son, Jesus Christ, would not come into condemnation but enjoy eternal life with God (John 5:24). What is still more, once reconciled to God, man would be introduced even here on earth into the majestic purpose which God originally had in mind when he created the universe.

Of that purpose we shall have more to say presently; but for the moment let us pause to concentrate on the centrepiece of God's salvation activity for mankind in history—the suffering, pain and death of Christ himself upon the cross. For, if this is really God, as the New Testament claims it is, then God has not remained distant from human suffering but has himself become part of it. And it is precisely this fact of the nearness of God that can begin to cut through the tears and anguish and bring the suffering person real hope. Not of some simplistic solution to their pain but of the possibility of coming, in spite of that pain, to have the confidence that Christ the Son of God understands their suffering and so can be trusted for the future.

Before we leave the topic of the suffering and death of Christ, we should make sure that we are clear about the conditions attached to God's offer of reconciliation through that death. The whole package of salvation is a gift; it does not have to be earned or merited in any way. But the conditions for receiving it are:

First, repentance towards God (Acts 20:21). 'Let the wicked forsake his way, and the unrighteous man his thoughts; and let him return to the LORD, that he may have compassion on him, and to our God, for he will abundantly pardon' (Isa 55:7).

Second, faith in the Lord Jesus Christ (Acts 20:21). 'Truly, truly, I say to you, whoever hears my word and believes him who sent me has eternal life. He does not come into judgment, but has passed from death to life' (John 5:24).

But with this we are back with the question of man's free choice. God will not force anyone to believe. He will not remove a man's free will, not even in order to save him. For if he did, the end product would not be a saved and glorified human being but a robot.

On the other hand, with all his heart God beseeches men and women to be reconciled. There is no reluctance to save on his part (1 Tim 2:3–6):

> In Christ God was reconciling the world to himself, not counting their trespasses against them … we are ambassadors for Christ, God making his appeal through us. We implore you on behalf of Christ, be reconciled to God. For our sake he made him to be sin who knew no sin, so that in him we might become the righteousness of God. (2 Cor 5:19–21)

If, in spite of that, man uses his free will, not only to turn from God in the first place, but then in addition to reject the forgiveness and redeeming love of God, how can God be blamed for the resultant disaster?

But now we must turn to that other source of suffering, namely, natural disasters, and to what we have broadly called the problem of pain.

CHAPTER 6

The problem of pain

There is no need here to list again the many natural disasters to which our planet earth is subject from time to time. Nor can we shut our eyes to the destructive effect which they have on human life and property. One thinks of the havoc caused in recent years by the earthquakes in Japan and Turkey, or by the floods in Bangladesh and Eastern Europe, by the famines in Ethiopia and the hurricanes in Haiti and the southern United States.

However, we should not overlook the fact that the more science discovers about our planet, the more astoundingly remarkable it turns out to be.

Our astounding planet

In the first place, it supports life! And not just life, but intelligent life, minds that can turn round on the universe and begin to understand how it works, and to ask how it all began, and what the ultimate purpose is for its existence. Why does it exist at all? How long will it last? When will it end?—and indeed, why does it suffer what we call natural disasters?

The eminent mathematical physicist, Professor Paul Davies, does not appear to believe in God as depicted in the Bible. But the sheer existence of intelligent minds on our planet moves him to write as follows:

> I cannot believe that our existence in this universe is a mere quirk of fate, an accident of history, an incidental blip in the great cosmic drama. Our involvement is too intimate. The physical species Homo may count for nothing, but the existence of mind in some organism on some planet in the universe is surely a fact of fundamental significance. Through conscious beings the universe has generated self-awareness. This can be no trivial detail, no minor by-product of mindless, purposeless forces. We are truly meant to be here.[1]

It is not as if planets capable of sustaining advanced forms of life were common in the universe. Professor Carl Sagan was an ardent believer in the possibility that there could be intelligent beings on other planets in the universe. But even he estimated theoretically that only 0.001% of all stars could possibly have a planet capable of supporting advanced life (and this now appears to have been an excessively large estimate). After spending a lifetime of research and millions of dollars in trying to find evidence for the existence of such intelligent beings, he found none.[2]

1 *The Mind of God*, 232.
2 Information taken from Hugh Ross, 'Earth, the Place for Life', *The Creator and the Cosmos*, 131–4.

Indeed, none of the other planets in our own solar system are able to support advanced life. And when one considers the long (and ever increasing) list of conditions that we now know must be, and are, met by our planet in order to support life, the evidence becomes overwhelming that our planet has been carefully designed and engineered for the purpose.[3] From this too, it would appear that, to borrow Paul Davies' phrase, 'we are truly meant to be here'.

And then there is the fantastic complexity of the biochemical machinery in every cell of the human body. In their book *Cosmic Life Force* the Cambridge astronomer Fred Hoyle and the mathematician Chandra Wickramasinghe, writing about the basic enzymes necessary for life, remark:

> A simple calculation then shows that the chance of obtaining the necessary total of 2000 enzymes by randomly assembling amino acid chains is exceedingly minute. The random chance is not a million to one against, or a billion to one or even a trillion to one against, but p to 1 against, with p minimally an enormous superastronomical number equal to $10^{40,000}$ (1 followed by 40,000 zeros). . . . If all these other relevant molecules for life are also taken account of in

3 e.g., to have the light and heat necessary for life, the planet must revolve around a star (our sun is a star); but it must neither be too near the star, or else it would be too hot for human life to survive, nor too far from the star, else it would be too cold. Its rate of daily rotation must neither be too great, otherwise vast destructive winds would be generated, as on Jupiter, nor too slow, otherwise the temperature on the night side would become too cold, and on the day side too hot. Astrophysicist, Hugh Ross (pp. 138–45), lists 33 such examples of the exactitude with which our planet has had to be engineered for the purpose of supporting human life.

our calculation, the situation ... becomes doubly worse. The odds of one in $10^{40,000}$ against are horrendous enough, but that would have to be increased to a major degree. Such a number exceeds the total number of fundamental particles throughout the observed Universe by very, very many orders of magnitude. So great are the odds against life being produced in a purely mechanistic way . . . .[4]

Once more, then, overwhelming evidence points to the fact that our existence as human beings on planet earth is not the result of mindless forces. The occurrence from time to time of natural disasters, therefore, cannot wipe out this massive evidence (and much more besides) that both our planet and we ourselves have been deliberately designed. And that raises the obvious question: Who is the Designer?

The Bible, of course, says that God is; but that at once brings us back to the problem of pain: How can we believe that a world in which there are so many natural disasters has been created by an all-loving, all-powerful and all-wise, personal God?

Humanity's own attitude to pain

Let's begin, then, by thinking about the attitude which, God or no God, men and women in general take towards pain. It will not answer all our questions; but it will at least help us to view our problem in its proper proportions.

4 p. 134.

We can pass over quickly the obvious point that we do not regard all pain as bad. Some pain is preservative and therefore good. Catch your finger accidentally on the blade of a sharp knife, and the pain of the cut will make you involuntarily withdraw your finger and so prevent further damage.

Fear of pain can be preventative. Fear of getting burned stops us putting our hands into fire. Fear of contracting AIDS could even restrain some people from immorality. Such fear, therefore, is good.

Pain and suffering constantly evoke sympathy, compassion, concern and self-sacrificing devotion on the part of nurses, doctors, social workers and others and so builds up in these caring people a noble character which the mere pursuit of selfish pleasure and the determination to avoid pain and sacrifice at all costs would never produce. This too is good; and we all admire such people (though curiously the public pays them a pittance yet pays film and music celebrities a fortune).

But let us move on to consider the attitude that many people take towards the risk of serious injury, pain and even death. No normal person is prepared to suffer pain or death just for the sake of it. But thousands of normal people are willing to run the risk of quite serious injury, and sometimes death itself, for the sake of nothing more than sports such as rugby, Formula 1 racing, hang-gliding, snowboarding and mountaineering.

Ballerinas suffer severe pain in their feet; and the pain that gymnasts and athletes voluntarily endure as they push themselves through the pain barrier in the course of their training is notorious. But the human spirit urges them on to attain mastery of their bodies, and to achieve perfection, beauty and grace of movement; and they count the pain involved to be worthwhile.

But again, let us move on to still more serious things. No nation is obliged solely for the sake of sheer survival to engage in space exploration. Yet nations do engage in it knowing full well what the colossal risks are; and people still volunteer to train as astronauts and to go on space missions even though they are fully aware that others have already perished in similar missions.

The elemental forces of nature—fire, wind, wave, electricity, gravity, atomic power—are all vastly more powerful than man is; and being impersonal and mindless, they will destroy him without compunction if he mishandles them. Electricity will cook your dinner, or, if you make a mistake, electrocute you. It knows no forgiveness. And yet man, made in the image of God (whether he acknowledges it or not) and made to have dominion over the works of God's hands (see Gen 1:26-28; Ps 8:6) knows in his spirit that he, with his mind and intelligence, is infinitely more significant than the elemental forces of nature. From the earliest days, he has set about the process of discovering how to harness these forces and make them serve his purposes. Fire was harnessed early. With the invention of ships and sails, the wind and waves which without them would drown a man, were now made to convey him on his voyages of exploration and discovery. Nowadays even earth's gravity is harnessed and used to accelerate a man-made space probe towards earth, and then to fling it out into space, as a sling does a stone, on its way to some other planet.

Humanity's attitude to the cost of progress

This whole scientific enterprise of harnessing the elemental forces of nature has been a magnificent expression of the human spirit. The process carried enormous risks, and achievement has been bought at the cost of endless pain and countless lives. But in the judgment of most people the vast benefits that have accrued to the whole human race have outweighed and justified the cost in terms of pain and death.

Then we should notice another very significant thing. Harnessing elemental forces does not mean removing from them their essential power to inflict pain and death. Nor would one wish it so. Fire that lost its potential to burn, would no longer be useful. Electricity that could not fry you to a cinder, would no longer be able to perform many of the tasks which, when harnessed, it does perform. Laser beams can destroy human tissue; if they couldn't, they could not be employed in delicate eye surgery as nowadays they are. It means, of course, that use of these elemental forces always carries a certain amount of risk; but most people consider the risk of injury and death worth taking in light of the benefits to be had.

Airplanes can overcome the force of gravity. Their invention and improvement has cost thousands of lives; but we still fly in them, knowing the risk that if the airplane's engines fail, gravity will destroy both it and its passengers. Yet nobody that I know of would think of arguing that God ought to have created our earth without any gravity, or with much weaker gravity than it now has, so that when an airplane's engines failed, gravity did not cause it to crash.

If earth's gravity were much weaker than it is, the planet would lose its atmosphere and life would have been impossible in the first place.

To sum up so far, then. Left to themselves, and without being forced, people in all ages have thought it acceptable to risk, and actually to incur, a certain amount of grave suffering and death in the course of developing the potentials of their planet (and nowadays of other planets too), because of the great advantages to be gained by taking the risks necessarily involved in such progress. People generally do not admire the attitude that refuses to reach out for progress, for fear that it might involve suffering and pain.

But that would seem to imply that mankind cannot in all fairness complain if God's purpose in creating our planet and us human beings upon it, inevitably involved suffering, not only for man but for God himself as well, for the sake of conferring on man an infinitely glorious and eternal benefit.

God's purpose in creating the world

According to the Bible our earth was never designed to exist for ever; one day it will end (2 Pet 3:13–18; 1 John 2:17; Rev 20:11–21:1). But man, being spirit as well as body, will never cease to exist. Physical death does not put an end to him. He will exist somewhere and in some state, in heaven or hell, eternally.

Earth, therefore, was never designed to be mankind's permanent home. It was intended simply as a temporary stepping stone towards the achievement of a far greater purpose for man, which God had in mind before he even created our earth. That purpose involved two stages:

Stage 1   Man would be born into this world as one of God's creatures. He would be endowed with body, soul and spirit; with intelligence, language faculty, moral sense and God-consciousness. But for none of this would it be necessary for God to seek man's prior consent or even cooperation. Man would simply become eventually aware that he had been born and would gradually discover that he had these faculties.

Stage 2   Man would later be offered the opportunity to become, what he had hitherto not been, namely a child, and then a son, of God. But for this, man's willing consent and choice would be necessary.

To understand the progression between these two stages we must be careful to notice the difference in biblical terminology between a creature of God on the one hand and a child and son of God on the other. Popular religious thinking often confuses these two things, and speaks as if all human beings were children of God. But that is not true. God certainly loves all human beings, for he is their Creator and they are all his creatures; and in non-technical language we may rightly say that he looks after them in a fatherly way. But in biblical language, while all human beings are creatures of God, not all are children of God.

The classic statement of the situation occurs in John 1:10–13. It will be worth quoting it in full:

> He [that is, the Son of God] was in the world, and the
> world was made through him, yet the world did not
> know him. He came to his own, and his own people
> did not receive him. But to all who did receive him,
> who believed in his name, he gave the right to become
> children of God, who were born, not of blood nor of
> the will of the flesh nor of the will of man, but of God.

From this passage five things are very clear:

First, a human being is not automatically a child of God, as a result of being born into this world. To be a child of God he has to become one; and you cannot become what you already are.

Second, the condition for becoming a child of God is that one must receive Christ and believe on his name: it is to as many as receive him that he gives authority to become children of God.

Third, not all human beings become children of God, for the simple reason that not all receive Christ: he came to his own, and they that were his own people (that is ethnically, in other words, the majority of his Jewish contemporaries) received him not. And many today, of all nationalities, do not receive him.

Fourth, the process by which one becomes a child of God: what it is not. It is not the same process as that by which we are first conceived and then born into this world through our parents. Nor is it an operation which we can perform on ourselves by our own will power.

Fifth, the process by which one becomes a child of God: what it is. It is to be begotten by God, God puts his own life in us.

This last description, 'begotten by God', points clearly to the difference between creatures of God and children of God. God's creatures are made by him, God's children are begotten by him. Let's use an analogy. An electronic engineer cannot get a child by the same process as he uses to get a computer. He makes, or creates, the computer; but he has to beget the child. And, of course there is a vast category difference between his computer and his child. The computer might be highly sophisticated and able to perform wonderfully complicated operations far beyond the capability of the infant child. But the computer would not possess the engineer's life: the infant child would. And with that life the infant child would grow up to enjoy a relationship with his father, and an enjoyment of his father's life, love and fellowship, which the computer could never hope to enjoy.

This, then, was the magnificent purpose that God conceived in his heart even before he made the world: he wished for sons and daughters that could share his own very life and so understand him, enjoy him and he them, in a fellowship possible only in a father–son/daughter relationship of shared life. Let us hear it stated in biblical language:

> He [God] chose us in him [Christ] before the foundation
> of the world, that we should be holy and blameless
> before him. In love he predestined us for adoption as
> sons through Jesus Christ, according to the purpose of
> his will, to the praise of his glorious grace, with which
> he has blessed us in the Beloved. (Eph 1:4–6)

Here then is the true progress for mankind which God himself designed: from being born by physical birth into this temporary world as a creature of God, to becoming a child of God by spiritual birth while still in this world, so as to be able eventually to live in fellowship with God eternally in his world.[5]

A suffering God

The vastness of this project can be seen first of all by the fact that its achievement involved a change in the very Godhead itself. The one whom Christians call the second person of the Trinity was not always human. The Word, as he is called, was not always flesh. But he became flesh, became human, so that redeemed men and women might be spiritually incorporated into him, as a physical human body and its members are part of each other, (see John 1:1–2, 14; 17:20–26; 1 Cor 12:12–14). And becoming truly human he suffered, sinless though he was, just as we do; and by that very suffering was equipped to become our spiritual file leader on our pathway to eternal glory (Heb 2:17–18; 4:14–16; 5:7–9; 12:1–3). God is no static or unfeeling God!

'But what', says someone, 'has all this got to do with the problem of pain and suffering which we are meant to be discussing?'

Why, this! Becoming a child of God depends on a person's willing consent to receive Christ. For that reason (in addition to the other reasons we earlier discussed) man

---

5 Very different this from the miserable progress proposed by Darwinian evolution: from protozoon, by means of mindless, purposeless changes, to life doomed to eventual oblivion!

had to be created, at what we have called the first stage, with a genuinely free will. Yet, as again we have already observed, God in his omniscience foresaw that man right from the beginning would use his free will to set his own will against God's will, to disobey God, and to lead himself and the whole human race on a downward path away from God. God also foresaw that the only way of redeeming humans, and bringing them back and making it possible to proceed with stage two of the project, was for the Son of God, not only to become human himself but to offer himself as humanity's representative Redeemer and Saviour, to bear the colossal cost, suffering, pain and penalty of human sin, and thus as the Lamb of God to take away the sin of the world. God foresaw it, and for his own sake and for humanity's sake, the Godhead was prepared to undergo the suffering involved in achieving the project on which God's heart was set. The Lamb was foreknown before the project was begun, before in fact the foundation of the world (1 Pet 1:18-21).

Two observations flow from this

First, how vast must the benefit and the glory be both for God himself and for redeemed humankind, if God himself thought it worthwhile for the Godhead to be involved in the incarnation and then in the suffering of the cross in order to achieve it.

Second, intellectual answers to the problem of pain are necessary and helpful. But the thing that soothes the heart of believers and gives them the courage themselves to face whatever sufferings God may allow them to encounter, is the fact that God has not remained aloof. As we saw when we considered the problem of evil in the previous chapter, God has not set out to achieve his purpose by allowing them to suffer without suffering anything himself. Precisely because the Son of God has himself suffered, being tempted, he is now able to help believers when they in turn are tempted (Heb 2:18). And because God has given his Son to die for them, believers are taught by the Spirit of God to know and feel in the depths of their being that:

> He who did not spare his own Son but gave him up for us all, how will he not also with him graciously give us all things? . . . Christ Jesus is the one who died—more than that, who was raised—who is at the right hand of God, who indeed is interceding for us. Who shall separate us from the love of Christ? Shall tribulation, or distress, or persecution, or famine, or nakedness, or danger, or sword? . . . No, in all these things we are more than conquerors through him who loved us. For I am sure that neither death nor life, nor angels nor rulers, nor things present nor things to come, nor powers, nor height nor depth, nor anything else in all creation, will be able to separate us from the love of God in Christ Jesus our Lord. (Rom 8:32–39)

The consequences of humanity's rebellion at Stage 1

We must now turn back in our thinking to what we have called Stage 1 in God's project for humankind; for, according to the Bible it was humanity's rebellion at this stage that has resulted in much of the suffering in the world ever since.

We have said that Stage 1 was only the first necessary stepping stone towards the achievement of God's major purpose; but that does not mean that Stage 1 was of no particular value or significance in itself. On the contrary, the position and role given by God to man in relation to planet earth was, and still is, noble and magnificent in the extreme. Man was to be God's viceroy, made in the image of God, set over the earth and all its contents, as God's chief administrator, to develop earth and all its potentials. That was a marvellously challenging, exciting and responsible task, calculated to develop not only his technical abilities but also his moral character. In spite of humanity's rebellion and estrangement from God it still is; but done in unbroken and constant fellowship with the Creator and according to his moral directives, it could have turned the whole world into a paradise.

The biblical account has it that to start humanity off, God planted a garden at a certain spot on earth and put his newly formed viceroy there. That shows, however, that the rest of the planet was not a garden; and man's terms of reference would have obliged him and his descendants eventually to go out and develop the potentials of the whole planet over which God had given them dominion.

That task would not have been altogether without danger and possible pain, as we see from the fact that God in his foresight had provided man's body with various defence and repair mechanisms: an immune system, for instance, to resist disease, and a blood clotting system to repair wounds and stop fatal blood loss. All God's creation was good, as God himself pronounced it (Gen 1:31); but it was not all necessarily safe, unless handled properly.

But man rebelled. It was not that he immediately descended into vice: it was something far more fundamentally serious than that. He was tempted to think that life could be developed more intelligently, more beautifully and more satisfactorily, if he dared to be independent of God. He decided, as many do still, that God's warning, that certain attitudes and behaviour would lead to death, was restrictive nonsense; and he deliberately stepped outside moral and spiritual dependence on God.

When man did that, he was not dismissed from his role of manager of planet earth; but two great changes occurred.

First, creation was subjected by God to frustration (Rom 8:20).

Two metaphors are used to describe it. First, creation is likened to a woman in childbirth: creation labouring in pain in order to bring forth the splendid result which under humanity's tending she was designed to produce. But she has never been able, so far, in spite of her pain and humanity's efforts, fully to produce it. That is because, secondly, creation, like a slave, is subject now to the bondage of corruption (Rom 8:20–22). The Bible hastens to explain that this condition, imposed on nature, is not to last forever. One day creation would be set free, and realize her full potential and reach her glorious goal.

But when man foolishly grasped at independence of God, it was for man's good that he should be made aware of the folly of his attitude. The world after all was not his. He did not invent it. It belonged to his Creator. If creation's frustrations, frustrated him and caused him pain and sorrow to the point where he repented and turned to God, that would be a good and healthy thing.

Chest pains in our bodies that warn us that our heart is sick and needs attention are good! And if creation's frustrations and groaning constantly remind the world that humankind is in rebellion against God and needs to be reconciled to him, that is good as well.

Second, man himself was subjected to death (Gen 2:17; 3:17-24).

Disobedience to the Creator and alienation from the source of life inevitably changed man himself, his attitude to God, and his attitude to creation. It also brought him decline, ageing and eventual death at every level. Lovely as much of creation continued to be, glorious as humanity's physical, emotional, aesthetic, intellectual and practical life at its best still is, man had to learn by experience that man shall not live by bread alone but by every word that proceeds out of the mouth of God (Deut 8:3; Matt 4:1-4). To have all the delights of a painless paradise without personal fellowship with God, even if it were possible, would be a spiritual disaster.

But, of course, it is not possible. Humanity's alienation from the Creator, and our disobedience to the Creator's moral commands, has perverted humans as administrators and stewards of earth's resources and elemental forces. The result is that often (though of course not always) it is not the inherent danger of earth's elemental forces, nor natural disasters by themselves, that bring pain and death to the greatest number, but humanity's perverse use of those forces and resources. Take a few examples.

In this century man discovered how to split the atom, and then how to induce nuclear fusion. That was a brilliant achievement of humanity's scientific intellect. But the first use humans made of this discovery was to destroy hundreds of thousands of our fellow human beings. Thereafter for several decades East and West built thousands of atomic warheads at enormous cost, ruinous to their economies, and threatened each other with them. Had they been used, it could have led to a vast, worldwide, natural disaster, if not the complete devastation of the planet. Now unused and idle, these decaying warheads and atomic power stations have proved to be both actual and potential sources of hideous human malformations, sicknesses and death.

In recent decades famine killed thousands of Ethiopians. In the West, however, the application of advanced scientific methods to agriculture had resulted in the production of great mountains of cereals, meat and butter, which were not needed and were stored up unused in specially built warehouses. But when people were dying in their thousands in Ethiopia, the European countries for a long while refused to give any of these vast amounts of surplus food to save Ethiopians from dying of famine, in case it should upset their economies!

The leading nations spend prodigious sums of money on armaments in the hope that the threat to use them may deter aggression. If only the nations could trust each other, they could invest this money in ridding earth of its poverty, plagues and deserts. But they cannot and dare not trust each other. So the poverty, plagues and deserts remain, while enormous sums of money, intellect and time continue to be employed in producing ever more sophisticated weapons.

The industrial processes of our modern world produce harmful emissions of chemicals that are creating a hole in the ozone layer and threatening to produce global warming, which if unchecked will lead to severe worldwide natural disasters. In spite of that, some of even the rich countries refuse to undertake to reduce these harmful industrial emissions; the insatiable consumerism of their people will not allow them.

We do not know whether in fact it is possible to have a planet like ours without the internal forces and processes that lead to the shifting of earth's tectonic plates and to occasional earthquakes and volcanoes. What we can see clearly is that this world would be far nearer the paradise it could be if it were not for the sinful perversion of humanity's stewardship and development of earth's elemental forces and resources.

God's program for the restoration of creation

But there is hope! Real solidly based hope! The Bible affirms that creation's subjection to frustration is only temporary: one day 'creation itself will be set free from its bondage to corruption' (Rom 8:21).

Indeed, the restoration has already begun. For when man in his blindness murdered Jesus Christ, the author of life, the Son of God himself, God raised Jesus Christ bodily from the dead. That resurrection carries implications for the whole of creation.

The risen Christ, says the Bible, is the firstfruits of them that have fallen asleep (that is, have died). The harvest will comprise all the redeemed of every century from the beginning of time (1 Cor 15:20–28). Creation itself shall be delivered from the bondage of corruption (Rom 8:21). There shall eventually be a new heaven and a new earth (2 Pet 3:13; Rev 21:1). And who knows how many further projects the God of all ingenuity and creative power will embark on thereafter?

'But why do we have to wait so many centuries for this promised restoration to happen?' says someone. 'Isn't the real reason that the promise was never anything more than the wishful thinking of religious people?'

Well, that's certainly not the reason which the Bible itself gives for the delay. It says that what the restoration of creation is waiting for is 'the revealing of the sons of God' (Rom 8:19). What use would it be for God to restore creation and then put it back into the hands of the same kind of weak and sinful human beings as before? In other words, creation is waiting for the completion of what we have earlier called *Stage 2* of God's project: for the production of children of God, and then their development into fully grown up sons of God (Col 1:28; 1 John 3:1–2), fit to take over and run the administration of the new heavens and the new earth as Christ's executive Body (Col 1:13–20; Eph 1:9–10, 19–23).[6]

The first step in this process is, as we earlier saw, that human beings having been created by God, should then become children of God. When that happens it does not mean that they are thereafter exempt from the suffering that those who are not children of God normally

6 Note that the Apostle Paul is not using the term 'sons' in a gender-exclusive sense but in a technical one that reflects the status that first-born sons had in the society his readers knew. We follow that usage here.

experience. 'And not only the creation, but we ourselves, who have the firstfruits of the Spirit, groan inwardly as we wait eagerly for adoption as sons, the redemption of our bodies', says the Bible (Rom 8:23). They may, in fact, find that becoming children of God additionally involves them in suffering persecution and even death for Christ's sake (John 15:18–16:4; 1 John 3:13–16), as has happened so very often to Christians all down the centuries in totalitarian countries. What is more, there is an additional problem for believers, and that is the disproportion of sufferings' distribution.

Disproportionate suffering

Whether it is suffering that comes from man's evil and unjust behaviour towards his fellow man, or suffering that comes from accident, illness or natural disasters, some people suffer vastly more than others. It is not merely the suffering by itself that overwhelms them but the sense that it is grossly unfair that they should suffer so much and others so little. 'Why me?' they say.

The Bible, of course, recognizes the problem and recognizes also that this is an aspect of suffering that tests the faith, even of believers in God, to the limit. The writer of Psalm 73, for instance, was a believer in God; but he admits (vv. 2ff.) that his faith in God's justice almost collapsed when he observed that all too often evil, unscrupulous, violent men prosper, become wealthy and have few health problems, whereas many good people suffer enormously by comparison (vv. 3–4). Similarly, the man whose story is told us in the Old Testament book of Job was a believer in God and a person of exemplary character and social concern. Yet he suffered an extraordinary succession of natural disasters, loathsome diseases and excruciating mental and physical anguish beyond what even wicked people normally experience. His faith in both the love and justice of God was almost completely destroyed, though in the end it triumphed.

Now the Bible does not call attention to these problems without having answers to give. But we should notice two things. The Bible does not attempt to give a full and final answer to these problems now. In the nature of things, such an answer cannot be given until the whole of history with its almost infinite complexities comes to an end, and the details of each person's case can be considered in the light both of life's total context and of its visible eternal results. And secondly, while the Bible gives us some answers that satisfy our intellects meantime, it concentrates more on answers that speak to our hearts; for the Bible's main aim in this context is to buttress our faith in God and to maintain our courage until God's ways with us are fully explained and vindicated at the final judgment. (Remember the beginning of chapter 5 and what the parents had to do for the girl suffering from a faulty spine?)

Of course, answers that speak to the heart will prove effective with people who have already experienced the love of God in Christ as a reality before they encounter severe suffering. They will not necessarily have any weight with atheists whose unbelief has never allowed them any personal experience of Christ's love. But that merely exposes the bleakness of the atheists' position, which forces them to accept that the disproportionate distribution of suffering is simply one more irrational effect of a basically irrational, amoral, and ultimately unjust and hopeless universe.

With believers it is otherwise. When it comes to the unjust suffering inflicted on them by evil men, they dare to rely on God's promise, guaranteed by his character and affirmed by the resurrection of Christ, that there is going to be a final judgment where all wrongs shall be put right. Like the writer of Psalm 73 they consider the final end of evil men, and, in spite of the believers' sufferings and the apparent prosperity of the wicked, believers would not even now change places with them for anything (Ps 73:17ff).

Moreover Christians are not surprised when they find themselves suffering at the hands of evil men enormously more than ordinary citizens do—as happens in many countries still. For Christians know it from the start that they are called upon to follow the example left them by Christ who 'committed no sin, neither was deceit found in his mouth. When he was reviled, he did not revile in return; when he suffered, he did not threaten, but continued entrusting himself to him who judges justly' (1 Pet 2:22–23).

Confident that at the final judgment God would see to it that justice was done, Christ accepted suffering from evil men; and more than that: he prayed for his executioners and suffered the penalty of sin at the hands of God for them that all might be saved, if they would.

Christians are therefore called in their turn to suffer for Christ their Saviour's sake as they declare boldly their faith in him, and to suffer for their fellow men's sake as they take God's offer of peace and forgiveness to a world that at heart is hostile to God. But Christians do not find such suffering a cause for doubting God's love or his justice: they find it a confirmation of Christ's forewarning (John 15:18–16:4) and an honour (Matt 5:10–12; Acts 5:40–42; 1 Pet 4:12–14).

But what about the other kind of suffering that comes not from evil men, but from natural causes, accidents, disasters, ill health, bereavement and such like things? The Bible does not explain why some believers suffer disproportionately far more than others. What it does do is, to take a most extreme case, that of Job's suffering, and point out how God allowed and used his suffering to demonstrate that his faith was genuine, to purify and strengthen it, and then to enlarge it. Faith, the Bible explains, is like gold (1 Pet 1:6–7). A valuable lump of genuine gold may nonetheless have impurities in it; a goldsmith will therefore put it through the heat of his crucible in order to remove the dross. The lump of gold will then be more valuable still. So faith needs to be demonstrated as unfeigned and genuine (2 Tim 1:5). It needs also to be purified so that we love and trust God for his own sake and not merely for the benefits which we receive from him (Job 1:9). In addition faith can vary in quantity (little or great, see Matt 14:31; 15:28) and in quality (weak or strong, see Rom 4:19–20). And like muscles in the human body faith grows and develops by being exercised and tested in increasingly difficult situations. God does not explain to us why he puts some of his people through what seems to us to be disproportionately severe testings: only the coming eternity will reveal that, when the results of that testing are revealed. All testing of faith, the Bible assures us (1 Pet 1:7), mild or severe, will be discovered to have produced praise, glory and honour, when Jesus Christ is revealed at his second coming. But the greater the test, the greater the glory and honour.

Here on earth a trained first aid worker does a very valuable job; but he is not put through such severe examinations as a student surgeon. Every few months airline pilots are placed in a simulator where they are put through every conceivable kind of hair-raising emergency situation to test their skills until even strong men break down in tears. But no one troubles even to question why their testing has to be so vastly greater than that of a would-be car driver. According to Christ, position and responsibility in his coming kingdom will depend in part on a disciple's suffering here on earth (Mark 10:37-39). The greater the suffering, the greater the eventual position of responsibility.

The best approach to the problem of suffering

In these last two chapters we have spent a long time—too long, some would feel—trying to face and to think through the many problems connected with suffering. But the best approach is not to try by ourselves to solve all our problems first and then to come to our Maker and put our faith in him. Rather we should come and put our faith in our Maker first, and then let him help us to think through our problems.

The Bible, in a helpful metaphor, tells us that we are all like sheep who need a shepherd. And our Maker has provided us with the Great and Good Shepherd who laid down his very life for the sheep. Now risen from the dead, he guarantees to all his sheep eternal security far beyond the few short years of our life on earth (John 10). He knows how to 'anoint our heads with oil, to lead us through the valley of the shadow of death without fear of evil, and to bring us at last to dwell in the house of the Lord forever' (Ps 23). Meanwhile nestling close to him we shall find rest to our hearts and soothing for our sorrows even while we must wait for the final answers to our problems.

A final contrast

We have pointed out several times that atheism can offer no hope. But the atheist's position is worse than that. His refusal, or inability, to believe in God does not mean that God does not exist. The atheist believes that death ends everything for the individual: that there is no afterlife. But his belief does not make it so. Death does not mean extinction. After death comes the judgment (Heb 9:27-28). Christ died so that all who repent and believe may be saved and enter God's heaven at last. But he did not die needlessly. To die unsaved is not the end of suffering: it is the beginning of the eternal anguish of being shut out from the presence of God forever. Suicide is most definitely not the answer to suffering. For the unbeliever death is, according to Christ himself, the doorway to eternal pain (Luke 16:19-31). In the nature of things, it could not be otherwise.

By contrast, for the believer suffering, of whatever kind, is never merely destructive: it is, as we have seen, one of the processes by which God develops those who have become his children into the moral and spiritual maturity of full-grown sons of God (Heb 12:1-13; Jas 1:2-4; 1 Pet 1:6-7).

There is no need to pretend that believers enjoy suffering; but they learn to adopt the attitude expressed by the Christian Apostle, Paul:

> So we do not lose heart. Though our outer self is wasting away, our inner self is being renewed day by day. For this light momentary affliction is preparing for us an eternal weight of glory beyond all comparison, as we look not to the things that are seen but to the things that are unseen. For the things that are seen are transient, but the things that are unseen are eternal.
> (2 Cor 4:16–18)

Moreover, for a child of God physical death takes on a different aspect. Believers do not enjoy the process of dying, and they have no need to pretend they do. But they do not fear death itself nor what it leads to. Christ for them has broken the fear of death (Heb 2:14–15); for them to depart from the body is to be present with the Lord (2 Cor 5:1–8).

The believer, therefore, is in the best position to see what life's true values are and to act upon them. There are some values in this life that are more important than physical life itself. Supreme among them is loyalty to the truth, to the Creator, to the Son of God, to the Holy Spirit and to all the moral and spiritual implications that flow from it. It is the man who believes that there is nothing after physical death that will be tempted to compromise what he knows to be true for the sake of clinging to life.

Believers in Christ take seriously the reality of a future resurrection of their bodies, just as Christ's body was raised, from the dead (cf. 1 Cor. 15). And Christ's resurrection, as we have noted already from the Apostle Paul's words (Acts 17) is God's guarantee to the world that there will one day be a day of judgment. Of course, some people find the very idea of Christ's resurrection from the dead to be laughable, while yet others feel they don't know enough about it and would like to hear more, just as they did in Paul's day (Acts 17:32). For both groups, and because of the seriousness of the implications of this central claim of the Christian gospel, we will now consider some of the evidence for the resurrection of Christ.

CHAPTER 7

The evidence for the resurrection of Christ

If the keystone is removed from an arch, the arch will collapse. The whole existence of the arch depends on the keystone. In the same way, the whole of Christianity depends on the resurrection of Christ. If the resurrection did not happen, if the New Testament's records of it could be proved untrue, then the whole of Christianity would collapse. Nothing worthwhile could be salvaged from it.

We can see that ourselves, if we read the New Testament and observe how central the resurrection is to its preaching and teaching. But what is more significant is that the early Christians themselves were aware that if the resurrection of Christ was not a fact, then there was nothing in Christianity worth having. Take, for example, the Apostle Paul. Writing to his converts in Corinth he says: 'If Christ has not been raised, your faith is futile and you are still in your sins' (1 Cor 15:17).

It is easy to see why this is so. Central to Christianity is the gospel. The gospel, says the Bible (Rom 1:16), is the power of God unto salvation. But how does it work? By offering and effecting forgiveness of sins, reconciliation and peace with God, through the death of Christ on the cross. But the death of a mere man could not make atonement for the sins of the world. Only one who was the Son of God could do that. Now Jesus predicted not only that he would die for our sins, but also that he would rise again. His resurrection would finally prove he was the Son of God. But suppose Jesus did not in fact rise from the dead. His prediction would then be shown to be fake. We could no longer believe he was the Son of God. We should then have to regard his death as simply one more cruel death such as many men have suffered. In that case Jesus' death could not procure forgiveness of sins for mankind any more than any other man's death. Christianity would be left with no gospel to preach.

Again, Paul says about himself and the other Christian apostles and preachers:

> And if Christ has not been raised, then our preaching is in vain and your faith is in vain. We are even found to be misrepresenting God, because we testified about God that he raised Christ, whom he did not raise if it is true that the dead are not raised. For if the dead are not raised, not even Christ has been raised. (1 Cor 15:14–16)

Here Paul tells us bluntly that if it were not true that Christ rose from the dead, he, Paul, and the other apostles would be convicted of being deliberate and despicable liars. For at the heart of their Christian gospel was their insistence that God had raised Jesus bodily from the dead, and that they had personally met, seen and spoken to him after his resurrection. How could anyone respect, let alone have faith in, Christianity, if its first propagators were a bunch of deliberate liars?

Some people suggest that if Paul were living today he would not insist on Christ's literal and physical resurrection, for he would know that many modern scientists and philosophers hold the theory that physical resurrection is impossible. But this suggestion is false. In the passage cited above, Paul tells us that many philosophers and scientists in his own day held a similar theory that resurrection (of anyone at all) is simply impossible. Paul was fully aware of their theory. But he held that the sheer historical occurrence of Christ's resurrection, witnessed by many responsible eyewitnesses, himself included, outweighed—and in fact destroyed—the mere theory of the contemporary philosophers and scientists. But if, knowing all about the scientists' theories, Paul and his fellow apostles had deliberately concocted a story of Christ's resurrection, aware in their own hearts that they had not seen, handled and talked to the risen Christ, and that it was simply a myth which they themselves had fabricated; then they were nothing but religious hoaxers, worthy of contempt. And the Christian gospel would stand in ruins.

In light of this, it becomes important to know who it was that first told the world that three days after his burial, Christ's tomb was found to be empty.

Not the Christians but the Pharisees

Notice what is recorded in Matthew's Gospel:

The next day, that is, after the day of Preparation, the chief priests and the Pharisees gathered before Pilate and said, 'Sir, we remember how that impostor said, while he was still alive, "After three days I will rise." Therefore order the tomb to be made secure until the third day, lest his disciples go and steal him away and tell the people, "He has risen from the dead", and the last fraud will be worse than the first.' Pilate said to them, 'You have a guard of soldiers. Go, make it as secure as you can.' So they went and made the tomb secure by sealing the stone and setting a guard. . . . While they were going, behold, some of the guard went into the city and told the chief priests all that had taken place. And when they had assembled with the elders and taken counsel, they gave a sufficient sum of money to the soldiers and said, 'Tell people, "His disciples came by night and stole him away while we were asleep." And if this comes to the governor's ears, we will satisfy him and keep you out of trouble.' So they took the money and did as they were directed. And this story has been spread among the Jews to this day. (Matt 27:62–66; 28:11–15)

From this passage we see that it was the Jewish authorities who first let it be known that Christ's tomb was empty. The Christians as yet said nothing to anybody (except among themselves); and it was to be another fifty days before, on the Day of Pentecost, they publicly proclaimed that Jesus had risen from the dead (see Acts 1 and 2).

Why then did the Jews act before the Christians and announce the fact that the tomb was empty? *Because it was a fact!* And, as Matthew tells us, they had strong reasons for not trying to cover up the fact: what would Pilate have said if fifty days later he had discovered that the Jewish authorities had been involved in a cover-up? And they had urgent reasons for getting their explanation of the fact across to the public and gaining credence for it at once, if possible. For they knew that the Christians would presently claim the empty tomb as evidence that Jesus had risen from the dead. They felt they must get out ahead of the Christians: the first explanation on the market, would, they hoped, gain the most credence.

Now the Jewish authorities' explanation of the fact is self-evidently untrue. It is impossible to believe it. But that still leaves the fact of the empty tomb. How shall it be explained?

The records of the resurrection were written by Christians

Would it not be more convincing, some people say, if some of the records of the resurrection were written by non-Christians? At least, they would not be biased and prejudiced; and therefore their independent witness would be more impressive.

Perhaps so. But there are the following considerations. First of all, in those early days people who became convinced that Jesus had risen from the dead, became Christians. It would be difficult indeed to find someone who was convinced of Christ's resurrection and yet did not become a Christian and so was able to give an 'unbiased' record of the evidence for the resurrection. The important thing to notice about the thousands who in those early days became Christians is that they were not Christians when they first heard the claim that Jesus was risen from the dead. It was the force of the evidence of his resurrection that converted them.

The conversion of Saul of Tarsus is a case in point:

> But Saul, still breathing threats and murder against the disciples of the Lord, went to the high priest and asked him for letters to the synagogues at Damascus, so that if he found any belonging to the Way, men or women, he might bring them bound to Jerusalem. Now as he went on his way, he approached Damascus, and suddenly a light from heaven shone around him. And falling to the ground he heard a voice saying to him, 'Saul, Saul, why are you persecuting me?' And he said, 'Who are you, Lord?' And he said, 'I am Jesus, whom you are persecuting. But rise and enter the city, and you will be told what you are to do.' The men who were travelling with him stood speechless, hearing the voice but seeing no one. Saul rose from the ground, and although his eyes were opened, he saw nothing. So they led him by the hand and brought him into Damascus. And for three days he was without sight, and neither ate nor drank. (Acts 9:1–9)

The case of Saul of Tarsus is special in many ways. But it is clear from the narrative that he was not only not a Christian: he was a positive and violent opponent of Christianity, and was out to destroy what he regarded as the fraudulent story of Christ's resurrection. But then the risen Christ appeared to him on the Damascus road. It was the reality of the risen Christ that converted him.

One cannot deny the historicity of his conversion. It was he who as the Apostle Paul did more than any other by his missionary travels, preaching and writings to establish Christianity in Asia and Europe. It was his writings that later transformed Europe at the time of the Reformation. And still to this day his writings exercise an enormous influence over millions of people. One cannot, therefore, ignore Paul's conversion; its effects have been so vast and so enduring. What, then, caused his conversion? He says that it was a personal encounter with Jesus after he rose from the dead; and, not surprisingly, his subsequent sermons and writings are full of the reality, the wonder, and the glorious implications of Christ's resurrection. If that resurrection was not in fact a reality, what other adequate cause can we posit for Paul's conversion?

But to get back to the question: why are there no records from the non-Christian contemporaries of the early Christians in support of the claim that Jesus rose from the dead? That question, as we have now seen, is rather unhelpful. A better question would be: where is the evidence from the contemporary opponents of Christianity that Christ had not risen from the dead? Many people at the time, of course, when they heard the Christians say that Christ was risen, immediately dismissed it from their minds as nonsense. Many still do. But the Jewish authorities in Jerusalem could not afford to do so. They had instigated his judicial murder; and in the first few weeks after Pentecost, when the Christians were daily proclaiming in the temple that Jesus was risen from the dead, and some few thousands in Jerusalem, including many priests, were getting converted, the authorities understandably made strenuous efforts to strangle Christianity at its birth (see Acts 2-9). They put the Christian apostles on trial, beat and imprisoned them, and tried (unsuccessfully) to suppress all preaching in the name of Jesus.

Then why did they not, in those first few weeks, do the one thing that would have stopped Christianity dead in its tracks? Why did they not produce the dead body of Jesus and put it on public display? They had all the panoply of State, including torture and help from the Roman governor, available to them to track down the body of Jesus if the Christians had, in fact, surreptitiously removed it. Why, then did they not produce the body?

'Because', said the Christians, 'they couldn't. The body was gone. Jesus had in actual fact been raised from the dead.'

Now the absence of this particular piece of negative evidence is surely significant. But in addition we must next ask: what kind of positive evidence did the first Christians put forward for the resurrection? To that question we shall now turn.

Exhibit A: **Physical evidence**

We first consider evidence from one of Christ's disciples, John. He says that when he first heard that the body of Jesus was missing from the tomb, he went at once to examine the situation. He found that though the body was indeed gone, the tomb was not completely empty: the grave clothes in which Jesus had been buried were still there. Furthermore, there was something about the positioning and state of the grave clothes that convinced him that the only satisfactory explanation of what he saw was that a miracle had taken place and Jesus had risen.

Now, many of us will have read detective stories or else followed closely the evidence in the trial of some well-known person. Even if we are but amateurs, we can use our detective skills on the evidence that John gives us. But first let us assess the reliability of John as a witness.

The reliability of John as a witness

The question is: can we be sure that in reporting what he saw, John is being honest and not deliberately telling untruths? So let us ask: What motive would he have had for lying? He himself reports that on the evening of the day in which he found the tomb empty, he and his fellow disciples met in a room that was bolted for fear of the Jews (John 20:19). A few weeks later he was twice imprisoned and then beaten by the authorities for publicly preaching that Jesus was risen from the dead (Acts 4:1–21; 5:17–42). Then his fellow Christian, Stephen, was stoned to death (Acts 6:8–7:60). Later his own brother, James, was executed by King Herod for his belief in the risen Christ; and so severe was the general persecution that many Christians were obliged to flee for their lives from Jerusalem (Acts 11:19; 12:1–2). During the subsequent persecution by the emperor Nero, many Christians suffered horrible deaths. And in his old age John himself was exiled on the island of Patmos (Rev 1:9). Are we to think, therefore, that having convinced many people of the resurrection of Jesus by telling lies about what he saw in the tomb, he was prepared to stand by and see them persecuted and executed for the sake of these lies which he had concocted; and then himself suffer imprisonment, fear of death, and exile for what he knew to be a lie?

Moreover a few pages earlier in his book (John 18:37) he records Christ's words before Pilate: 'For this purpose I was born and for this purpose I have come into the world—to bear witness to the truth. Everyone who is of the truth listens to my voice.' Is it likely that shortly after writing this, he deliberately falsified the record of what he saw in the tomb in order to bolster the claim of Jesus to be witness to the truth? If he did, he was a most despicable religious charlatan. But religious charlatans don't write books of moral power and spiritual beauty like the Gospel of John. You may think John was mistaken or self-deceived over what he saw in the tomb; but it is impossible to think that he is was deliberate liar.

So let us now investigate (a) what he tells us about the way Jesus was buried; (b) what he saw in the tomb on the third day after the burial; and (c) what he deduced from what he saw. Then we shall be in a position to make up our own minds.

The way Jesus was buried

After these things Joseph of Arimathaea, who was a disciple of Jesus, but secretly for fear of the Jews, asked Pilate that he might take away the body of Jesus, and Pilate gave him permission. So he came and took away his body. Nicodemus also, who earlier had come to Jesus by night, came bringing a mixture of myrrh and

> aloes, about seventy-five pounds in weight. So they
> took the body of Jesus and bound it in linen cloths
> with the spices, as is the burial custom of the Jews.
> Now in the place where he was crucified there was
> a garden, and in the garden a new tomb in which no
> one had yet been laid. So because of the Jewish day of
> Preparation, since the tomb was close at hand, they
> laid Jesus there. (John 19:38–42)

From these verses and from John 20:1 (and from Luke 23:53) we learn that Jesus was buried not in a grave dug in the earth, but in a tomb hewn out of the rock face. The entrance to the tomb and the space inside were big enough, we learn (John 19:40, 42 and 20:6–8), for at least two adult people to enter, in addition to the corpse. The dead body would not have been laid on the ground but on a shelf hewn out of the wall of the tomb. The mixture of myrrh and aloes which Nicodemus brought would have weighed at least 25 kg. This is not an exaggerated, fairy tale figure, but usual for the burial of an honoured and valued personage in the ancient Middle East.[1] Both the myrrh (a fragrant resin) and the aloes (made of aromatic sandalwood) would have been used in powdered form. The body of Jesus was wrapped in strips of linen cloth, interlarded with the spices. The head (see John 20:7) was bound round with a large face-cloth which, running beneath the jaw and then over the top of the head and

1 About 35 kg of spices were used by a certain Onkeles at the funeral of the Rabbi Gamaliel a little later in the first century AD ('Onkelos and Aquila' in *Encyclopaedia Judaica*, 2007) and, according to Josephus, a much larger quantity was used at the funeral of Herod the Great just before the start of the first century (*Antiquities of the Jews*, 17.8.3).

round the front and back of the head, would have kept the jaw from falling open. The body would then be laid on the stone bench, at one end of which there would have been a shallow step to act as a cushion for the head.

What John and Peter saw in the tomb

Now on the first day of the week Mary Magdalene came to the tomb early, while it was still dark, and saw that the stone had been taken away from the tomb. So she ran and went to Simon Peter and the other disciple, the one whom Jesus loved, and said to them, 'They have taken the Lord out of the tomb, and we do not know where they have laid him.' So Peter went out with the other disciple, and they were going toward the tomb. Both of them were running together, but the other disciple outran Peter and reached the tomb first. And stooping to look in, he saw the linen cloths lying there, but he did not go in. Then Simon Peter came, following him, and went into the tomb. He saw the linen cloths lying there, and the face cloth, which had been on Jesus' head, not lying with the linen cloths but folded up in a place by itself. Then the other disciple, who had reached the tomb first, also went in, and he saw and believed; for as yet they did not understand the Scripture, that he must rise from the dead. (John 20:1–9)

It is clear that Peter, John and Mary Magdalene, in spite of all that Jesus had told them, were not expecting Jesus to rise from the dead. Otherwise, they would have been at the tomb to see it happen; and on finding the tomb empty, Mary would not have reported the fact to John in the words: 'They [some unknown persons] have taken away the Lord out of the tomb and we don't know where they have placed him.' And even when Peter and John heard Mary's report, they still did not grasp the implication that the Lord had risen from the dead, and explain it all to Mary. They simply ran to investigate what had happened. Grave robbing was a common practice at the time (the Roman Emperor Claudius, AD 41–54, issued a decree—a copy of which, engraved on stone, has been found in Palestine—forbidding it on pain of death). It could, for all Peter and John expected, have been that grave-robbers had removed the large stone that would have been used to cover the entrance of the tomb once the body had been placed inside, and had stolen the body in the hope of finding jewellery and other small valuable items buried with it (not to speak of the large amount of very expensive spices bound up with the extensive—and valuable—linen cloths).

Now when John first arrived at the tomb, he tells us that he did not go in, but peeped in from the outside. From that position the thing that immediately caught his eye was that, though the body was gone, the grave clothes were still there. The next thing that struck him forcibly (he mentions it twice, in v. 5 and again in v. 6) was that the grave clothes, that is the linen cloths, were not only there: they were lying there. That is, they were not in a heap, they were not thrown all round the tomb (as they might have been if robbers had hastily torn them off the body); they were lying there still on the shelf just as they had been when the body was inside them, but flattened somewhat now that the body was gone.

Then Peter caught up with John, and in his character-istically impetuous manner (notice how uncontrived and true to life the narrative is) entered the tomb, and John with him. Now they could both see, what from outside the tomb John could not see, the position of the face-cloth that had been round Christ's head.

The immediately noticeable thing was that it was not lying with the linen clothes. It was twirled round upon itself just as it had been when it had been on the Lord's head; and it was lying by itself in a distinct place, presum-ably on the shallow step that had served as a cushion for the Lord's head.

What John deduced from what he saw

He saw and believed, says the narrative. Believed what? Not simply believed what Mary had told them about the body being missing. It would not have taken the presence, position and state of the linen cloths and the face-cloth to confirm Mary's story. John could just as easily have seen that the body had gone, if the grave-cloths had gone as well. Nor, so he tells us, did what he saw remind him of Old Testament Scriptures that indicated that the Messiah must rise from the dead, and so lead him to conclude that these Scriptures must have been fulfilled. At the time, he says, neither he nor Peter had realised that the Old Testament prophesied that Messiah must rise again. And what is more, he had not yet met the risen Lord, and did not do so until the evening of that day.

What he deduced from the presence, position, and state of the linen cloths and the face-cloth was that the body of Jesus had come through the grave clothes without unwrapping them, and had left them largely undisturbed, though somewhat collapsed. In other words a miracle had taken place. Christ's body had somehow gone and left the grave clothes behind. A resurrection, whatever that might turn out to mean, had taken place.

The reasonableness of John's belief

We can say at once that what John saw shows conclusively that the body had not been removed by grave robbers. They would not have taken the body and left the grave clothes and spices which were worth more than a dead body. And had they undone all the linen cloths and the face-cloth in order to get the body out, they would not have delayed in order to put the cloths back again just as they were before the body was taken; not when there was a posse of soldiers on guard outside, liable any moment to inspect the tomb (see Matt 27:62–66).

But suppose the impossible, that someone, friendly to Jesus, had managed under the very noses of the soldiers to break the seal on the tomb and roll away the stone, intent on removing Jesus' body for religious or sentimental reasons. It is conceivable that they would have removed the grave clothes from the body so as not so easily to be seen to be carrying a dead body through the streets. It is also conceivable that they might have put the grave clothes back to make it look to the soldiers on a casual inspection as though the body was still there. But they would not have left the stone rolled away and the tomb wide open! And we know from Matthew that when the soldiers did look into the tomb, they were not deceived into thinking that the body was still there (Matt 28:11–15). But all this unlikely speculation founders on the fact that if anyone friendly to Jesus had removed the body and buried it elsewhere for safekeeping, they would eventually have told the other disciples where it was.

So next suppose that someone had taken the body away and deliberately arranged the grave clothes to make it look as if a miracle had taken place. Who would that someone have been? The authorities in Jerusalem would certainly not have done any such thing. And, for reasons which we discussed at the beginning of this chapter, neither John, nor any other of the early Christians, would have perpetrated such a deceit; nor could have done with a posse of soldiers on guard.

Final conclusion

What John and Peter saw, then, when they went to the tomb early on the first day of the week, constitutes a powerful piece of physical evidence for the resurrection of Christ. And there was more to follow. In the evening of that same day Christ appeared to his disciples in the upper room, showed them his hands and his side (John 20:30); got them to handle him to see that he was not a disembodied spirit, but a body with flesh and bone; and called for food and ate it in their presence (Luke 24:36–43), and continued to appear to them in similar fashion for the next forty days. This cumulative physical evidence confirmed John's initial deduction from the grave clothes, and made the resurrection of Christ, not merely a theory that could be deduced from lifeless physical evidence, but a personal experience of the living Lord.

But now we must investigate another kind of evidence for the resurrection.

Exhibit B: Psychological evidence

We cite here the striking fact that in the whole of the New Testament (as distinct from later decadent centuries) there is not the slightest hint that the early Christians venerated the grave of Christ or made a shrine of his tomb. This is remarkable, for the Jews of the time were in the habit of venerating the tombs of their famous dead prophets (see Luke 11:47-48); but the Christians built no shrine around Jesus' grave, nor made it a special place of pilgrimage or prayer. Nowhere in the New Testament is there the faintest suggestion that a visit to Jesus' tomb was of some spiritual benefit or efficacy. When from time to time in the course of his missionary journeys the Apostle Paul returned to Jerusalem, we read of his calling on the Christian leaders, of his visiting the Jewish temple, of celebrating Pentecost, but never of his paying a visit to the tomb of Christ.

And this is all the more remarkable because in the hours that followed the Lord's burial, the Christian women began to behave in a way that if unchecked would naturally have led to turning the tomb into a shrine of prayer and devotion to Christ. But something checked them. What was it? What power or influence was strong enough to overcome the natural psychological instincts that impel people, and women in particular, to cling to the relics of loved ones now dead? And what was it that stopped dead any superstitious tendency to imagine that the tomb of Christ possessed magical powers?

A reconstruction of events

All four Gospels are unanimous that the first Christians to visit Christ's tomb on the third day after his burial were a group of women from Galilee. Out of gratitude for what Christ had done for them, these women had followed him on his long, slow journey to Jerusalem, and had helped and supported him from their own resources. They could afford to do so, for they were comparatively well off. One of them, indeed, a certain Joanna, was the wife of a man called Chuza, who was the manager of King Herod's household (Luke 8:3). When Jesus was crucified, they stood watching at some distance from the cross along with others of Christ's acquaintances (Luke 23:49). And when he was buried by Joseph and Nicodemus, both wealthy men, these well-to-do women from Galilee were not afraid to join the little burial procession. They saw what tomb he was buried in, noted exactly where it was, and how the body was positioned in the tomb. They watched Nicodemus wrap 25 kg of aromatic spices in with the strips of linen that were bound round the body. But large and expensive as that amount of spices was, it was not enough for them. They wanted to express their own love and devotion to Christ. So they went back to the various places in Jerusalem at which they were staying over the Passover period (Joanna may well have been staying, with her husband, in Herod's Jerusalem palace); and there they prepared more spices and ointment (Luke 23:55-56). Their intention was to return to the tomb as soon as the Sabbath day was over and reverently and affectionately anoint the body of Jesus still more.

But at this point we meet a difficulty that has caused many people to conclude, after a superficial reading of the gospels, that their accounts of the resurrection of Christ contradict each other. That is not so. The difficulty arises simply because none of the gospel writers sets out to record everything that happened. Each writer selects from his particular sources what particularly interested him and fits it into the flow of his particular narrative; and in so doing he naturally omits or telescopes other events. But if we collect all that the four gospels between them say about the women from Galilee, we can with care compile a coherent account of what they did and where they went on the day in question. The story goes like this:

When, at early dawn on the first day of the week, they arrived at the tomb, they were startled to find the stone already rolled away from the entrance (Luke 24:1-2). Some of them entered—they could scarcely have all got inside at once—and immediately shouted their alarming discovery to the others, that the body was gone. Whereupon Mary Magdalene did not wait to see what happened next—which was that after a while two angels appeared to the women inside the tomb and told them that Christ was risen (Luke 24:4-8). Mary ran off at once as hard as she could to the house where John and Peter were staying. Breathlessly she reported what seemed to her the obvious explanation, that someone or ones had removed the body from the tomb and that neither she nor the other women knew where they had deposited it. Thereupon, Peter and John immediately ran to the tomb. From the presence, state and position of the grave clothes John concluded that a miracle had taken place: Christ must have risen from the dead; and with that, he and Peter went back (directly or indirectly) to the house where they were staying, and waited to see what would happen next (John 20:1–10).

Mary, however, went back to the tomb. The other women, of course, had gone. They had in fact been so scared by the appearance of the angels and by the message the angels ordered them to take to the apostles that for a while they told nobody about it (Mark 16:8). Presently joy got the upper hand over fear, and they started out to go to the apostles, when the risen Lord met them and confirmed the message they were to convey (Matt 28:9–10). Whereupon they proceeded, not like Mary had done to the house where John and Peter were staying, but to a small upper room in Jerusalem which the (now eleven) apostles had hired as a place to meet in. There the women told their amazing story to the apostles who by this time had been joined by John and Peter.

Let's leave them there for a while and rejoin Mary. This is what happened as she stood looking into the tomb.

> But Mary stood weeping outside the tomb, and as she wept she stooped to look into the tomb. And she saw two angels in white, sitting where the body of Jesus had lain, one at the head and one at the feet. They said to her, 'Woman, why are you weeping?' She said to them, 'They have taken away my Lord, and I do not know where they have laid him.' Having said

this, she turned around and saw Jesus standing, but she did not know that it was Jesus. Jesus said to her, 'Woman, why are you weeping? Whom are you seeking?' Supposing him to be the gardener, she said to him, 'Sir, if you have carried him away, tell me where you have laid him, and I will take him away.' Jesus said to her, 'Mary.' She turned and said to him in Aramaic, 'Rabboni!' (which means Teacher). Jesus said to her, 'Do not cling to me, for I have not yet ascended to the Father; but go to my brothers and say to them, "I am ascending to my Father and your Father, to my God and your God."' Mary Magdalene went and announced to the disciples, 'I have seen the Lord'—and that he had said these things to her. (John 20:11–18)

Consider the following points:

1. Mary had originally come to the tomb that morning with the other women from Galilee to honour the body of Christ. Dead though it was, she could not let it go. She would express her love to the Lord as she anointed his body with costly ointment, and stifled the smell of the corpse with her fragrant spices.

2. Distraught at finding the body gone, her one thought now was to regain possession of it: though she did not refer to the body as 'it'; to her the dead body was still 'him'. It was all she now had of him. 'Tell me', she said to the man whom she supposed was the gardener, 'where you have laid him and I will take him away.' For it was unbearable to her not to know where the body was and to be left with not even a relic of it, and not even a grave that she could venerate as his.

3. Suppose, then, the 'gardener' had showed her where the body was and she had taken it away. What would she have done with it? There is no doubt. She and the other women would have bought for it, or rather, him, the best tomb obtainable, no expense spared. Lovingly they would have buried him; and his grave would have become for them the most sacred place on earth. They would have made a shrine of it, venerated it, and visited it as often as they could.

4. But something happened to Mary that day in the garden that blew all such ideas clean out of her heart and head once and for ever. It must have been something very powerful to banish so completely and suddenly all the former psychological instincts and reactions. What was it?

5. It was that in the garden that day she encountered the living Lord Jesus, risen from the dead. Of course she abandoned the tomb! You don't venerate the tomb of someone who is alive and whom you have just met! You don't go to a tomb to pray to someone with whom you can have a direct living conversation!

6. But there was more to it than that. Mary's previous experience of Jesus had been wonderful; but death seemed to have destroyed it, leaving her nothing but a dead body: fragrant memories but a blighted heart. Now Jesus did a wonderful thing. He replaced that earlier experience with an utterly new, warm, vibrant, living relationship between Mary and God the Father, between Mary and himself, a relationship bound together by a life that not even Mary's eventual physical death could possibly destroy. 'Go tell my brothers', said he, 'I ascend to my Father and your Father, to my God and your God.' Thereafter though still on earth, Mary knew herself bound to God and Christ in heaven by

the indestructible power of eternal life already possessed, entered into, and enjoyed. So did all the other disciples. And so may all today who confess Jesus as Lord and believe in their hearts that God has raised him from the dead.

In her new-found life and ecstatic joy Mary now went to convey the risen Lord's message to the other disciples. And this time she went, not to the house where John and Peter were staying, but to the upper room. There she reported to the Eleven and all the others that she had seen the Lord (Luke 24:10; John 20:18). That was more, of course, than Peter or John or any others of the Eleven had so far done; and Peter, much perplexed went off to examine the tomb once more (Luke 24:12). It was shortly after that—and before Christ appeared to all the apostles at once in the upper room—that he appeared to Peter (1 Cor 15:5, here called Cephas). The painful matter of Peter's recent denial of the Lord had to be cleared up: and it was better done in private.

After this the early Christians showed no further interest in the tomb where the body of Christ had lain. They had no reason to visit it—they knew that Jesus had risen.

Exhibit C: The evidence of the Old Testament

The writers of the New Testament tell us honestly that when on various occasions the disciples saw the risen Lord, some doubted (Matt 28:17). Sometimes the reason why they hesitated to believe was that it seemed too wonderful, too joyful, too good to be true. They did not want to believe it uncritically, only to find that it could not survive hard-headed examination (Luke 24:41). And then a miracle the size of a resurrection, when they first heard about it from the women who claimed to have met the risen Lord, seemed more likely to be the result of over-heated imagination than hard, objective fact. But that kind of reluctance to believe was eventually swept away by the sheer concrete, tangible evidence of the risen Lord inviting them to touch him, sitting bodily with them and eating an ordinary meal (Luke 24:41–42).

But there was another form of unbelief, the cause of which ran deeper and had to be removed by somewhat different methods, as we shall now see:

> That very day two of them were going to a village named Emmaus, about seven miles from Jerusalem, and they were talking with each other about all these things that had happened. While they were talking and discussing together, Jesus himself drew near and went with them. But their eyes were kept from recognizing him. And he said to them, 'What is this conversation that you are holding with each other as you walk?' And they stood still, looking sad. Then one of them, named Cleopas, answered him, 'Are you the only visitor to Jerusalem who does not know the things that have happened there in these days?' And he said to them, 'What things?' And they said to him, 'Concerning Jesus of Nazareth, a man who was a prophet mighty in deed and word before God and all the people, and how our chief priests and rulers delivered him up to be condemned to death, and crucified him. But we had hoped that he was the one to redeem Israel. Yes, and besides all this, it is now the third day since these

things happened. Moreover, some women of our company amazed us. They were at the tomb early in the morning, and when they did not find his body, they came back saying that they had even seen a vision of angels, who said that he was alive. Some of those who were with us went to the tomb and found it just as the women had said, but him they did not see.' And he said to them, 'O foolish ones, and slow of heart to believe all that the prophets have spoken! Was it not necessary that the Christ should suffer these things and enter into his glory?' And beginning with Moses and all the Prophets, he interpreted to them in all the Scriptures the things concerning himself. (Luke 24:13–27)

The reason for the travellers' disillusionment

The two travellers on the road to Emmaus were disillusioned; and the reason was this. On our Lord's last visit to Jerusalem they had joined the large crowds who had genuinely thought that Jesus was the Messiah, whose coming was promised by God through the Old Testament prophets. Now from their (probably scant and superficial) knowledge of the Old Testament, they were expecting that the Messiah, when he came, would turn out to be a powerful military and political leader who would raise armies and lead the nation of Israel in a successful uprising against the imperialist forces of the Roman occupation. 'We hoped', they explained to the stranger who joined them on the road, 'that he was the one who would liberate Israel.'

But, of course, Jesus had done no such thing. Far from liberating the masses of Israel, he had been arrested, tried, condemned and crucified by a combination of the Jewish religious establishment and the Roman military governor. And the mockery that had gone on at the trial had made a public laughing-stock of Jesus' claim to be a king. At one blow the whole movement had come to nothing, like a pathetic, ill-organised, ineffectual peasant rising. What good was a political liberator who could not even save himself from being crucified? So the two travellers were going home in profound disillusionment.

Why at first could they not take in the fact that Jesus had risen from the dead? It was because, to their way of thinking, Jesus had not fulfilled the Old Testament's promises of a coming Liberator–King. Instead, he had been defeated, crucified, a failure. He was therefore not the promised Messiah. And that being so, the rumour that he had risen from the dead seemed not only incredible in itself but irrelevant into the bargain. If he wasn't the Messiah, what was the point of his being raised from the dead?

So what had to be done to make faith in the resurrection possible for them? Notice that at the beginning of his conversation with them the risen Lord did not attempt to convince them that he was Jesus. Indeed he first gently chided them because their reading of the Old Testament had been unduly selective. They had read the parts that appealed to them, about the promised coming of a Liberator–King. But they had overlooked, or not understood, or conveniently forgotten the parts that foretold that the Messiah would first have to suffer and die, and only after that would be raised from the dead and enter his glory. And so the stranger took them through the whole Old Testament and pointed out passages that either stated, or else clearly implied, this. The point of the lesson was obvious: if the Old Testament prophesied that Messiah must first suffer and die, then Jesus' sufferings and death, far from proving that he was not the Messiah, were strong evidence that he was. If, in addition, the Old Testament prophesied that after his death Messiah would live again and liberate his people and share with them the spoils of a great victory, then to do that he would have to rise from the dead.[2] The reports which the two travellers had heard from the women that Jesus was risen and that they had seen him, might therefore be true after all. The stumbling-block that had prevented their believing was removed.

The relevance of this incident to us

Still for us today one of the most important strands of evidence for the resurrection of Christ is that the Old Testament foretold, not only that the Messiah would rise from the dead, but that he would do so as an integral part of God's plan for the redemption of mankind. Notice the repeated emphasis on this fact in the Apostle Paul's great statement of the Christian gospel:

> For I delivered to you as of first importance what I also
> received: that Christ died for our sins in accordance

2 See the implication in Isa 53:8–12 that the Messiah would first suffer and die, and then rise from the dead. Likewise see Psalm 16 and compare with Acts 2:25–32.

> with the Scriptures, that he was buried, that he
> was raised on the third day in accordance with the
> Scriptures. (1 Cor 15:3–4)

A report that some otherwise unheard-of ordinary individual had been raised from the dead unexpectedly and for
no apparent reason might well be difficult to believe. We
should all ask: 'Why him?' and 'What is the point of it?' and
'How can we believe that such an extraordinary exception
to the laws of nature has taken place arbitrarily and for
no apparent reason?' Atheists, of course, believe that the
universe as a whole has come into existence for no apparent reason. Its existence cannot be accounted for: it is just
an arbitrary, inexplicable, brute fact. Those who believe in
an intelligent Creator, however, would find it difficult to
believe that the Creator had overruled the normal laws of
nature arbitrarily to raise some obscure individual from
the dead for no apparent reason.

But Jesus was no ordinary person! He was God incarnate. Nor was his resurrection an isolated phenomenon. It
was part of the Creator's gigantic plan for the redemption
of mankind and for the eventual renewal of the universe.
Nor was the story of the resurrection invented by Christ's
disciples. God had had it announced through his prophets
and written down in the Old Testament centuries before
Jesus was born into our world. And it is still open to us
today to study the Old Testament seriously and see for
ourselves whether the birth, life, death and resurrection
of Christ match the Old Testament's God-given prophecies.

When Jesus had finished his rapid survey of the Old
Testament, the main difficulty in the way of the travellers'

believing was removed. But they still did not recognise that the stranger was in fact Jesus risen from the dead. How, then, did they come to recognise him? We must look at that in detail because it raises a large general question.

How did they know it was really him?

What evidence convinced the disciples that the person who appeared to them claiming to be Jesus risen from the dead was actually Jesus and not some kind of impersonation?

> So they drew near to the village to which they were going. He acted as if he were going farther, but they urged him strongly, saying, 'Stay with us, for it is toward evening and the day is now far spent.' So he went in to stay with them. When he was at table with them, he took the bread and blessed and broke it and gave it to them. And their eyes were opened, and they recognized him. And he vanished from their sight. They said to each other, 'Did not our hearts burn within us while he talked to us on the road, while he opened to us the Scriptures?' And they rose that same hour and returned to Jerusalem. And they found the eleven and those who were with them gathered together, saying, 'The Lord has risen indeed, and has appeared to Simon!' Then they told what had happened on the road, and how he was known to them in the breaking of the bread. (Luke 24:28–35)

The two travellers invited the stranger to stay the night with them, and they sat him down to an evening meal. But still they had not recognised who he was. Then he took the bread that was on the table, gave thanks, broke it and began to give it to them. And in that instant their eyes were opened and they recognised him; and he vanished out of their sight. Later, when they returned to Jerusalem and recounted their experience, they explained that Jesus was recognised by them when he broke the bread.

What was there so special about his breaking of the bread? First, in taking the bread, breaking it, giving thanks and giving it to them in their own house, he was taking over the role of the host. That must have riveted their attention on him. Second, in that moment as he broke the bread they would have caught sight of the nail-prints in his hands. But there was more to it than that. Watching those hands break the bread the way he did, it would have evoked memories of what only the closest of Jesus' disciples could have known about. They would have heard from the eleven apostles before they left for Emmaus how at the Passover meal on the night he was betrayed Jesus has taken bread, broken it and uttered what then must have sounded very mysterious words, but words which no one ever had said to them before: 'This is my body which is given for you.' There had followed the (for them) devastating experience of the cross. But now they had listened to the stranger's exposition of Old Testament passages. These passages not only prophesied that Messiah would have to die and rise again, but also explained why: he would have to die for his people's sins, and indeed for theirs too. Now as they saw him with nail-pierced hands break bread and give it to them personally, his action carried profound overtones which no impersonator could have known about or invented. Its significance was utterly and uniquely peculiar to Jesus. They recognised him at once. It was unmistakably Jesus.

How do we know it was really him?

But what about those millions, like us today, who have never seen, and cannot see Jesus with our own two eyes?

> Now Thomas, one of the Twelve, called the Twin, was not with them when Jesus came. So the other disciples told him, 'We have seen the Lord.' But he said to them, 'Unless I see in his hands the mark of the nails, and place my finger into the mark of the nails, and place my hand into his side, I will never believe.' Eight days later, his disciples were inside again, and Thomas was with them. Although the doors were locked, Jesus came and stood among them and said, 'Peace be with you.' Then he said to Thomas, 'Put your finger here, and see my hands; and put out your hand, and place it in my side. Do not disbelieve, but believe.' Thomas answered him, 'My Lord and my God!' Jesus said to him, "Have you believed because you have seen me? Blessed are those who have not seen and yet have believed.' (John 20:24–29)

Notice that Jesus did not rebuke Thomas for doubting. He respected his honesty. Jesus did not rebuke Thomas for demanding evidence before he would believe. And Jesus gave Thomas the evidence he asked for.

This reveals an interesting and important thing. Jesus had obviously heard Thomas speak and heard his demand for evidence even though Thomas was unaware of his presence at the time; for when he entered the room, without waiting for Thomas to say anything, he offered him the evidence he had earlier demanded.

That reminds us that at this very moment because Jesus is risen from the dead, he hears what we say and knows what we are thinking. And we may certainly express ourselves freely and say, if we really mean it: 'If Jesus is really alive, let him provide me with evidence that I can really believe; and then I will believe on him.'

But before we do so, let us ponder deeply what else Jesus said to Thomas: 'Because you have seen me, you have believed; blessed are those who have not seen, and yet have believed.' Evidence that can be seen with physical eyesight is not the only kind of evidence available that Jesus is alive. If it were, physically blind people could never see it. It is not, in fact, by itself the best kind of evidence. The evidence that is perceived by our conscience, heart and spirit, is far and away the best evidence. And no one ever speaks to our hearts like Jesus does. He says that he personally loves us and died for our sins according to the Scriptures, and has risen again according to the Scriptures; and that if we open our hearts to him, he will enter and fill them with his presence and love. If with conscience, heart and spirit we listen to him speaking the Bible to us as he did to the travellers, and if we come to see that his hands were nailed to the cross as he gave himself to death for us personally, we shall find that 'faith comes from hearing, and hearing through the word of Christ' (Rom 10:17). And we too shall find our hearts burning within us as he talks to us on life's journey and opens to us the Scriptures.

CHAPTER 8

The search for spiritual satisfaction

All of us crave satisfaction. We are built that way. Physical appetite, aesthetic taste, moral judgment, love—all alike cry out for satisfaction.

Often we get it, but often we do not. And when we do not, we feel frustrated, cheated, let down. We cannot reconcile ourselves to the idea that life was not intended to make sense. Reason will not be mocked by any such theory. Nor will our imaginations consent to be perpetually disillusioned. Science reveals everywhere the evidence of rational design and purpose. Imagination can see what a superb thing life could be if only people behaved reasonably and life went as it seems it was designed to go.

Then why doesn't it?

The quest for satisfaction

Why do people so often behave so unreasonably? Why are our dreams and expectations and well-laid plans so often frustrated by illness, or war, or faceless economic processes, or the imposition of somebody else's ideology? And come to that, why do I myself ruin my own chance of happiness by irrationally indulging in what I know will injure me and hurt those on whose love my happiness depends? Our very disappointment drives us to look for an answer. We cannot just resign ourselves to being constantly unsatisfied and progressively disillusioned. If we cannot be satisfied, then at least we look for some satisfactory explanation why not; why it is that life, so seemingly full of promise, so often goes wrong or sour. We want to know if there is any way of putting right whatever it is that's wrong; whether there is any way to eventual satisfaction.

Sooner or later we shall turn to religion. We know, of course, or at least we suppose we know, what it is going to say.

It will say that our basic trouble is sin.

That's perfectly true; but by itself it isn't likely to help us very much. It is like telling a man with cancer that his basic trouble is illness.

We all know that we are sinners. The question is, how are we to change, to eradicate the trouble, to stop the moral rot that threatens to eat away our happiness and frustrate any sense of satisfaction?

Again we know, or at least we think we know, what religion is going to prescribe: try harder to be good; be kinder, less selfish, purer; pray, deny yourself, discipline yourselves. All of it tough medicine. But then, if life is worth living at all, it is worth taking seriously.

So we make the attempt to take religion seriously, and attend scrupulously, perhaps over-scrupulously, to our religious duties.

Curiously enough, that does not always satisfy us either. And the reason probably is that we have simply been doing what we supposed our religion was telling us to do, but we have not stopped long enough to listen for ourselves to hear exactly what Jesus is saying to us, personally. He certainly can give us satisfaction, deep-running, permanent satisfaction, a well of living water within us, as he once described it (John 4:13–14), such that when we once have received it, we shall never lack satisfaction again. But to get this satisfaction, we shall first have to accept his diagnosis of our trouble, and then his treatment. Both are more radical than we may have imagined.

The satisfaction of being right with God

The basic dissatisfaction that underlies all other dissatisfactions that it is possible for the human heart to feel springs from this: our sins are an offence to Almighty God our Maker. They constantly fly in the face of his laws and provoke his wrath (Rom 1:18; 2:1–3; 3:19). He therefore withholds from us that sense of peace with God without which no creature of God can feel truly at ease or truly satisfied.

It follows that our first step towards satisfaction must be to be reconciled to God. The demands of God's holy law must be fully met. He must be completely satisfied that justice has been carried out, that never again will he need to direct his holy wrath upon us.

On our side, our sense of acceptance by God must be total, without reserve or uncertainty. Otherwise reconciliation is not true reconciliation.

To illustrate the point, the Bible tells the story of a reconciliation at the human level that was not full and unreserved, and was therefore unsatisfactory.

King David's son, Absalom, murdered his half-brother, Amnon, and in fear of the king's justice fled the country. Some three years later David's friends persuaded him to overlook the offence and allow Absalom to return from exile. The king, however, was not really happy about the justice of the thing; so he tried a compromise. Absalom was allowed back, but he was not allowed access into the king's presence; he was not allowed to see the king's face, as the Hebrew quaintly puts it. But half a reconciliation like that is not true reconciliation at all; and on this occasion it only led to further pretence, alienation and eventual disaster (2 Sam 13:23–18:33).

By happy contrast, when Christ reconciles us to God, God accepts and welcomes us without reserve. We can come into the presence of God at any time (Rom 5:2; Eph 2:18). We do not have to wait until we die to discover whether we shall be admitted into his presence or not. We can come at once, assured that God's wrath against us is a thing of the past (Heb 10:19-22), that there is no condemnation or rejection to be feared for the future (Heb 10:14-18; 1 John 4:17-19). The love of God casts out fear; the presence of God becomes our home. But the conditions are strict.

There must be on our side radical repentance towards God and faith only in what Christ has done for us and in nothing and no one else (Rom 5:9; 8:1; John 5:24). True repentance is not just admitting that things like pride and lying and impurity are wrong and sinful, nor simply determining to forsake these things. True repentance towards God means facing up to our true legal position in the light of the verdict which God passes on us in his Word. And it is at this point that it is so easy for us to be less than radical in our thinking, and therefore to be less than realistic in our attitudes, and therefore in the end to attempt superficial remedies that cannot bring satisfaction, because they satisfy neither God nor us.

We know we are sinners, and as such unacceptable to God. And so, with honest enough intention, we do what seems to us the obvious thing to do: we set about improving ourselves in the hope of eventually winning acceptance with God (Acts 20:21). Actually we are being seriously unrealistic in two respects.

First, the sins we have already done are in themselves enough to have deserved death and rejection by God. No amount of future improvement can wipe out the guilt of the past, or compensate for it, or buy off its deserved penalty.

Secondly, even if we started improving this moment (and let's hope we do), experience itself, let alone God's Word, warns us that by the end of life we shall not have improved enough to be accepted by God on the ground of our achievement. God's verdict on us then will still have to be what it is now: we have all sinned in the past, and in the present still come short of God's standard (Rom 3:23).

And that being so, God, for all his love, is not going to pretend that it isn't so; is not going to be satisfied with our inadequate efforts. As Ronald Knox's translation so plainly puts it: 'Observance of the law cannot win acceptance for a single human creature' (Gal 2:16).

That is very gloomy; but we might as well face reality. Satisfaction can hardly come by putting our heads in the sand. Our legal situation before God's justice is serious in the extreme. That is why, in order to effect a satisfactory reconciliation, God's justice had to take the extreme measure of handing over God's own Son to suffer the sanctions of God's law on our account. There was no other way. Had acceptance with God been obtainable on the ground of our improvement, Christ would never have died, would never have needed to. But it was not obtained that way, and Jesus had to die (Gal 2:20–21; 3:21–22; Rom 4:25; 8:32).

But from his death comes the greatest and most glorious news that man ever heard. What we could never have done, Christ's death has achieved for us. He has satisfied God's justice, he has paid the penalty of sin (2 Cor 5:20–21; Gal 3:13–14).

God can now accept, and with perfect, uncompromised justice accept, everyone who puts his faith in Christ and comes to God solely on the grounds of that sacrifice. God's acceptance of every such person is without reserve. Indeed God almost labours the point to show how completely and permanently accepted such a person is. He calls attention to the fact that Christ's death was followed by his resurrection, ascension and entry into the immediate presence of God. He then points out that Jesus came right into God's presence not on his own behalf only, but as the declared representative and forerunner of those who trust him. And God finally declares that all whom Jesus thus represents may know themselves accepted by God as fully and completely and finally as their represent-ative himself (Heb 6:17–20; 9:11–14, 24–28; 10:1–18; Eph 2:1–10).

In that lies the secret of profound and permanent satis-faction. To know oneself accepted by God like that, fully and for ever, is to have peace with God. And peace with God is the only secure foundation for true and lasting satisfaction.

The satisfaction of becoming what we were meant to be

To be accepted by God solely because of the sacrifice and death of Jesus sounds to many people, when they first hear about it, too good, or rather too easy, too slick, to be true.

It sounds as if you could go on sinning and it wouldn't matter: you could still be accepted by God simply because Jesus died for your sins and you said you believed in him. In other words, it sounds like a license to go on sinning with impunity.

Of course, it isn't true; though, interestingly enough, it is precisely what people said when they first heard the apostles preach the gospel (Rom 3:8, 31; 6:1–2, 15)—which shows that we must be on the right track; and we know the kind of thing the apostles said in reply.

It isn't true, because of what is involved in 'believing in' Jesus as Saviour.

Believing in Jesus does not mean simply assenting to the fact that Jesus died for our sins. It means committing ourselves without reserve to him as Lord.

More. It means receiving Jesus as a living person (John 1:12); it means becoming united with him by his Spirit (Rom 6:5); becoming 'one with him' (John 17:20-21; Rom 8:9-11); being joined to him (1 Cor 6:15-17) in a living spiritual partnership.

As we considered earlier (ch. 4), the nearest analogy to it in ordinary relationships is when husband and wife become 'one flesh', no longer completely separate and independent individuals, but a living union (Rom 7:1-4). And in this union with Christ lies the key to God's way of making us into what we were meant to be.

There can be no heaven, no final satisfaction, without becoming what God our Creator meant us to be, and behaving accordingly. That, of course, we instinctively realize. But God's way of making us into what we were meant to be is radically different from what we normally think it is.

We naturally think in terms of improving ourselves. We like to think of ourselves as basically sound, with a moral speck or two here, a bit of downright badness there maybe, spoiling the otherwise perfect decent apple. Our hope and expectation is that by the application of some religious discipline, perhaps even of some moderately severe spiritual surgery, we shall eventually become so improved as to be fit to enjoy, and make our contribution to, God's heaven.

But God does not think that way at all. The New Testament never talks of improving us or our old life or fallen nature.

God does something far more radical.

He implants within the believer a new life (1 Pet 1:23-2:3), which carries with it a new nature (2 Pet 1:4; Col 1:27; 3:3-4), with new powers and instincts, and new potentials. That is why in days gone by, when people became Christians, they took or were given a new name. Simon, for instance, was renamed Peter (John 1:42). The new name was not the expression of a pious hope that one day they might improve. It was the acknowledgement that Christ had given them a new life (Rom 6:4), a new power, a new nature, which they did not have before. The 'new self' or the 'new nature' (Col 3:10) or the 'new creation' (2 Cor 5:17)—these are some of the terms which the early Christians used for this gift of new spiritual life which they received through their union with Christ.

Receiving this new life did not mean that their old fallen nature disappeared and no longer made itself seen and heard. But receiving the new life was like dropping an acorn into a grave: it would not improve the corpse; but it would start growing a new life of its own which would gradually and eventually displace everything else.

So the believer in Jesus has no longer one, but two natures, the old and the new. He is called to constantly renewed decision and effort to 'put off the old' (Eph 4:22–23), to 'put it to death' (Col 3:5), not to 'let it reign' (Rom 6:12), and to 'put on the new, which is constantly being renewed [for that is a feature of life] in knowledge after the image of God its Creator' (Eph 4:24 own trans.).

It is, of course, the business and practice of a lifetime, constantly to put off the old and to cultivate the new. It is a struggle (Gal 5:16–17), a war in which we do not win every battle, but in which there is forgiveness for defeat (1 John 1:7–9), and certainty of final triumph (Rom 5:2; 8:29–30). In every believer the new life will grow and develop until it is finally conformed to the pattern of Christ himself.

What happens, we may ask, if, having received this new life, we neglect it, and instead encourage and indulge the old? And does it matter?

It matters indeed.

If we act in that way, God will discipline us. We must use our new spiritual powers to prevent the old fallen nature from taking control. If not, God will have to take more drastic steps. That may involve sickness, or even premature physical death. The matter is so important that Paul dwells on it at length in 1 Corinthians 11:23-32. The whole passage is important.

God's disciplines are solemn and serious. He will not allow us, if we are genuine followers of Christ (Heb 12: 3-11; Phil 3:10-14), to become smug, or cynical. Nor will he let us be satisfied with ourselves until God is satisfied with us. But notice that even in the extreme case where a believer is removed under God's discipline by physical death because of his careless living, the Bible explicitly says that he will not be condemned along with the world (1 Cor 11:32). The reason for that is that while our enjoyment of God, and God's enjoyment of us, depend upon our cultivation of the new life we have received through Christ, our acceptance with God never has and never will depend on our spiritual progress but only on what Christ has done for us by his death. Our acceptance, therefore, remains eternally secure.

This, then, is God's way of making us into what we were meant to be. It is the only effective and satisfactory way (Gal 1:8; Col 2:20-23).

The satisfaction of working as we were meant to work

It stands to reason that if God made us, and made us primarily (as the Bible says he did) to do his will and fulfil his pleasure (Rev 4:11; Col 1:16), we can never find satisfaction until we work as we were meant to work and fulfil the purpose for which God made us. That means, of course, giving up our own ways and thoughts wherever they differ from God's; it means for ever saying, 'Not my will, but thine, be done.'

Frankly, to many of us that sounds a bleak and dauntingly unattractive way of life.

We don't mind being moderately religious; but to 'take every thought captive to obey Christ', as Paul puts it (2 Cor 10:5), to consult Christ as Lord about all that we do in life, and to accept his control in everything—well, only a born saint, we tell ourselves, could contemplate living life like that; and even he, we suspect, could hardly enjoy it.

It is natural enough to think like that, perhaps. But it shows how, all unsuspecting, we have formed quite slanderous ideas about God, as if he were, if not a tyrant, then a killjoy. Think what we will about God, of course, it does not alter the fact that as his creatures it is our duty to serve him. But serving him merely out of a sense of duty is again less than satisfactory, and even if we manage to do it, it tends to induce in us a martyr spirit, an obnoxious attitude of the 'what a good boy am I' variety.

The only satisfactory and satisfying way of serving God, is to serve him willingly and gladly with all our heart, mind, soul and strength; more out of love than out of duty.

But how can it be done?

You can force yourself to serve God if you try hard enough; but you cannot make yourself love him. What then is the secret of loving and serving God as we were meant to love and serve him?

Paul tells us himself. It is a mixture of love and logic. When we begin to understand what Christ has done for us, not only does our gratitude affect the way we feel, it also has powerful implications for the way we live our lives. Paul, with his overwhelming sense of Christ's love for him personally, is compelled to see that:

> And the life I now live in the flesh I live by faith in the
> Son of God, who loved me and gave himself for me.
> (Gal 2:20)

And again:

> For the love of Christ controls us, because we have
> concluded this: that one has died for all, therefore
> all have died; and he died for all, that those who live
> might no longer live for themselves but for him who
> for their sake died and was raised. (2 Cor 5:14–15)

Paul had, so he tells us (Phil 3:4–6), always been religiously minded, but he had not always thought like that. In his early manhood he had thought that serving God was a way of storing up merit, and that this was a way of achieving salvation. And so he had gone in for serving God with immense thoroughness and determination. But all it managed to do for him—and it is he who says it of himself—was to pile up a load of religious works worth absolutely nothing and worse than nothing in God's sight (Phil 3:7–8), and to turn him into a proud, hard, cruel man (1 Tim 1:13; Acts 26:9–11).

The change came when he discovered who Christ really was, what Christ had actually done for him, and why it was he needed Christ to do it for him anyway. He discovered that far from being the religious success he thought he was, he was a wretched, despicable sinner. His supposed merits were objectionable rubbish, his religious exercises valueless; the law of God which hitherto he had imagined that he had kept, only condemned him.

And then he discovered Christ. He discovered who he was. This Jesus whom he had resented and persecuted in the name of God, was none other than God incarnate.

The discovery was shattering.

It exposed Paul's religiosity as being the expression of his own self-will; the boosting and serving of his own ego under the guise of religion, in actual (though hidden and unconscious) opposition to God.

Then he discovered something else about God's Son, and the discovery revolutionized the whole motivation of his life.

He discovered that even while he was his enemy, this Jesus had loved him personally and had voluntarily died for Paul so that Paul need not die under God's wrath.

The effect on Paul was unceasing gratitude.

But not just gratitude. Sheer logic made him see that had Christ not died for him, he must have died himself.

The life he now lived, therefore, he owed entirely to Christ. It was no longer his own; it belonged to Jesus, bought by the death that had redeemed him (1 Cor 6:19–20). It must therefore be lived entirely for Jesus. And he willingly and gladly lived it that way. Only so could Paul's love for Jesus be satisfied.

The next discovery that Paul made was that when in love and gratitude one submits one's life to the control of Christ, Christ's 'yoke' is in fact easy, as Jesus himself claims it is, and his burden is light (Matt 11:28–30).

Christ is, after all, our Creator. He knows how we were meant to work. His control and discipline is not a tyranny forcing us to live unnaturally; it is the control necessary to save us from ruining ourselves with the frustration of living perpetually at cross purposes with our Creator's design for us. It is the only way to true self-fulfilment, to living and working as we were meant to live and work.

And the other discovery that Paul made was that there is a great reward in serving Christ (1 Cor 3:11–15). The reward is not salvation, of course, or acceptance with God. Reward is for work done (1 Cor 3:14), whereas salvation is never the result of work done; it is given as a free gift (Eph 2:8–10).

The reward for working for Christ is first the sheer joy and satisfaction of knowing we have pleased the Lord (Matt 25:23). It is secondly the satisfaction of achieving something worthwhile and eternally significant (1 Cor 3:14; 1 Pet 5:4). And thirdly it is finding we have developed our potential to do greater and more significant work (Luke 19:16–17).

If Paul had a motto, I think it must have been this: 'For to me to live is Christ' (Phil 1:21). And when he came to die there was not the slightest regret. Nothing but satisfaction (2 Tim 4:6–8).

We might be tempted to think, of course, that Paul was such a saint that his experience is irrelevant to ours. But that is not so. He tells us himself that God designed his conversion as a pattern for everyone else's (1 Tim 1:16).

The satisfaction of knowing what is going on

Not to know what is going on can be very frustrating. To be asked or compelled to work in some scheme without being told what exactly the scheme is; to be expected to struggle and make sacrifices for it, without knowing whether the scheme is succeeding or not, whether the sacrifices will in the end be justified, or whether the whole thing will peter out in failure or end up in disaster— that is a tantalizing and unsatisfying way of carrying on.

Unhappily, that is how many people live, work and die. With life's lesser schemes and projects, their own plans and ambitions, they rightly try to define their goals, estimate their chances of success, decide whether success when achieved will be worth the effort put into achieving it.

But about the purpose of life itself, and what lies beyond life, and whether life's toils and sacrifices will in the end prove to have served some worthwhile eternal goal, or whether the whole of life will end in eternal disaster, on all this they have only the vaguest of ideas and the most uncertain hopes. Some even suppose that living in uncertainty is how we were meant to live anyway; that this is what faith means: to live courageously with uncertainty. But of course, faith in the biblical sense is the very opposite of uncertainty. 'Faith', says the Bible, 'comes from hearing, and hearing through the word of Christ' (Rom 10:17).

Faith, in other words, is our response to what God tells us. And if God tells us anything, the last thing in the world that we should be about it is uncertain. When we listen to Christ, then, he banishes uncertainty.

We discover in him not only the one *by* whom all things were made, but the one *for* whom all things were made (Col 1:16). He will inherit all things: the vast revenues of history will be his; he is the goal of all things (Heb 1:2). What is more, he does not keep us in the dark as to what his purposes are, either for us personally or for the world at large. Obviously, as finite creatures there is much about the world to come that we cannot be told, since we could not, in our present condition, understand it. But we are told a great deal, and certainly enough to satisfy faith, and to fill life with meaning and purpose.

'No longer do I call you servants,' says our Lord, 'for the servant does not know what his master is doing; but I have called you friends, for all that I have heard from my Father, I have made known to you' (John 15:15). So we are given to know that Jesus who went away from us at the ascension is to return. 'In my Father's house', he tells us, 'are many rooms. If it were not so, would I have told you that I go to prepare a place for you? And if I go and prepare a place for you, I will come again and will take you to myself, that where I am you may be also' (John 14:2-3). Here then we have that sure and certain hope of resurrection at the second coming of Christ, which is held out to us for our comfort and encouragement (1 Thess 4:13-18).

Death is not the final word; it shall not have the final victory (1 Cor 15:54-58). It does not reduce life to nothingness and therefore to ultimate insignificance. Christ will come again; and *Maranatha*—Aramaic for 'the Lord will come' (1 Cor 16:22) is the rallying watchword of every Christian.

Meanwhile, until that great event the individual believer is told what will happen to him personally at death. Like an expatriate who has been living away from home on business, but then when the business is done goes home, so the believer at death departs to be 'with Christ' (Luke 23:43; Phil 1:23; 2 Cor 5:6-8), to be 'at home with the Lord'.

That is tremendously comforting for the individual. But, wonderful as that is, God plans to do far more than save and make perfect individuals. Christ tells us that the whole of creation will be restored. Nature is not for ever to be chained to the frustration of corruption and decay. 'Creation itself', we are told, 'will be set free from its bondage to decay and obtain the glorious liberty of the children of God' (Rom 8:18-21). What that will mean in detailed practical terms we are not told, and doubtless could not understand in our present limited state. Nor does it matter. The great point is that the incarnation and the bodily resurrection of the Lord Jesus combine to tell us that matter is basically good. The world of nature is not an illusion, not a meaningless cycle from which, if we are wise, we shall try to escape.

The material world is God's own good idea. It has been temporarily spoiled by the rebellion of intelligent and morally responsible creatures against the Creator. But that condition is not to be permanent. Creation itself shall be reconciled and made to serve the Creator's will (Col 1:20). Matter will eventually function perfectly to the glory of God.

There is, then, a purpose within history, hidden maybe, but really there. Human effort is not ultimately in vain. The resurrection of Christ is described as the 'firstfruits' of a harvest. That harvest will include the resurrection of those reconciled to God. If we are believers, this will give us confidence to live and work to the full. For we know that what we do is not meaningless (1 Cor 15:58). Here then is satisfaction.

Let none say it is escapism. It implies that every decision, every action here in this life, is of eternal consequence. For the Christian it holds out the promise of life that now is and of that which is to come (1 Tim 4:8). For unbelievers it means that this life will in the end for ever prove to have been all too significant (John 3:36; Rev 21:8; Matt 12:36–37).

The way to satisfaction

In these chapters, we have considered whether Christianity is merely a drug to dull the pain of existence or the very truth of God by which we might know the author of life. That query now brings us, necessarily, to another: If there is spiritual satisfaction to be had, then how can I get it? We should be trifling with things if in the end we did not bring the whole matter down to this personal, practical question.

The answer is simplicity itself. 'Believe in the Lord Jesus, and you will be saved', says Scripture (Acts 16:30–31). But the very simplicity of it can be tantalizingly difficult. Do we not all, or most of us anyway, believe in some sense in Jesus?

In some sense, yes; but obviously, that believing which really receives from Jesus the satisfaction which he holds out to us, must somehow be a deeper, more real, more intimately personal thing than a superficial, general kind of belief in Jesus.

True faith, says the Bible (Rom 10:17), comes from hearing Jesus speak. Not, of course, hearing voices out of the blue; but listening to Jesus speak through the Bible, and allowing him by his Spirit to make his word a living, creative reality to us. For that very reason he has left us a recorded conversation which he had with a woman on this very topic of receiving spiritual satisfaction. Here is that story. Read it. Read it more than once. And as you listen to Jesus speaking to a woman all those centuries ago, pray that he will, by his Spirit, speak to you now. And he will (John 6:37):

> So he came to a town of Samaria called Sychar, near the field that Jacob had given to his son Joseph. Jacob's well was there; so Jesus, wearied as he was from his journey, was sitting beside the well. It was about the sixth hour.
>
> A woman from Samaria came to draw water. Jesus said to her, 'Give me a drink.' (For his disciples had gone away into the city to buy food.) The Samaritan woman said to him, 'How is it that you, a Jew, ask for a drink from me, a woman of Samaria?' (For Jews have no dealings with Samaritans.) Jesus answered her, 'If you knew the gift of God, and who it is that is saying to you, "Give me a drink", you would have asked him, and he would have given you living water.' The woman said to him, 'Sir, you have nothing to draw

water with, and the well is deep. Where do you get
that living water? Are you greater than our father
Jacob? He gave us the well and drank from it himself, as did his sons and his livestock.' Jesus said to
her, 'Everyone who drinks of this water will be thirsty
again, but whoever drinks of the water that I will give
him will never be thirsty again. The water that I will
give him will become in him a spring of water welling
up to eternal life.' The woman said to him, 'Sir, give me
this water, so that I will not be thirsty or have to come
here to draw water.'

Jesus said to her, 'Go, call your husband, and come
here.' The woman answered him, 'I have no husband.'
Jesus said to her, 'You are right in saying, "I have no
husband"; for you have had five husbands, and the one
you now have is not your husband. What you have
said is true.' The woman said to him, 'Sir, I perceive
that you are a prophet. Our fathers worshipped on this
mountain, but you say that in Jerusalem is the place
where people ought to worship.' Jesus said to her,
'Woman, believe me, the hour is coming when neither
on this mountain nor in Jerusalem will you worship
the Father. You worship what you do not know; we
worship what we know, for salvation is from the Jews.
But the hour is coming, and is now here, when the
true worshippers will worship the Father in spirit and
truth, for the Father is seeking such people to worship him. God is spirit, and those who worship him
must worship in spirit and truth.' The woman said to

him, 'I know that Messiah is coming (he who is called Christ). When he comes, he will tell us all things.' Jesus said to her, 'I who speak to you am he.' (John 4:5-26)

Bibliography

Bruce, F. F. *The New Testament Documents: Are They Reliable?*
Leicester: Inter-Varsity Press, 2000.

Craig, William Lane. *Reasonable Faith: Christian Truth and Apologetics*. [1984] 3d edn. Wheaton: Crossway, 2008.

Davies, Paul. *The Mind of God*. London: Simon & Schuster, 1992.

Documents of the 22nd Congress of the Communist Party of the Soviet Union, October 17-31, 1961. New York: Crosscurrents Press, 1961.

Habermas, Gary. *The Case for the Resurrection of Jesus*. Wheaton: Crossway, 2008.

Hoyle, Fred and Chandra Wickramasinghe. *Cosmic Life Force*. London: J. M. Dent, 1988.

Josephus. *Antiquities of the Jews*.

Kitchen, K. A. *On the Reliability of the Old Testament*. Grand Rapids: Eerdmans, 2003.

Knox, Ronald A. *The New Testament of our Lord and Saviour Jesus Christ*. London: Burns & Oates, 1945; repr. 1966.

Lewis, C. S. *Miracles: A Preliminary Study*. 1947; repr. London: Collins, 1974.

Lewis, C. S. and Walter Hooper (ed.). *Fern-Seed and Elephants and Other Essays on Christianity*. 1975; repr. Glasgow: Collins, 1982.

Bibliography

Lewis, H. D. and R. L. Slater. *The Study of Religions*. Harmonds-
worth: Penguin Books, 1966.

Moule, C. F. D. *Phenomenon of the New Testament*. Grand Rapids:
Kregel, 2004.

Popper, Karl. *The Open Society and its Enemies*. London: Routledge
& Kegan Paul, 1966.

Ross, Hugh. *The Creator and the Cosmos: How the Greatest
Scientific Discoveries of the Century Reveal God*. Colorado
Springs: Navpress, 1995.

Shaw, George Bernard. *Plays Pleasant and Unpleasant*, Vol. II. 1898.

Skolnik, Fred, and Michael Berenbaum, eds. *Encyclopaedia Judaica*,
22 vols. 2nd edn, Detroit: Macmillan Reference, 2007.

Turnbull, H. W. et al., eds, *The Correspondence of Isaac Newton*.
7 vols. Cambridge: Cambridge University Press, 1959–77.

Whitehead, Alfred North. *Science and the Modern World*. London:
Macmillan, 1925.

Zaehner, R. C. *The Concise Encyclopaedia of Living Faiths*. London:
Hutchinson, 1977

Scripture Index

General Index

Other books by David Gooding
(published by Myrtlefield House)

The Riches of Divine Wisdom (NT use of OT)
According to Luke (The Third Gospel)
In the School of Christ (John 13–17)
True to the Faith (Acts of the Apostles)
An Unshakeable Kingdom (Letter to the Hebrews)
How to Teach the Tabernacle
Windows on Paradise (Gospel of Luke)

Other books by John Lennox

God and Stephen Hawking: Whose Design Is It Anyway?
(Lion, 2011)
God's Undertaker: Has Science Buried God? (Lion, 2009)
Gunning for God: A Critique of the New Atheism (Lion, 2011)
Miracles: Is Belief in the Supernatural Irrational?
VeriTalks Vol. 2. (The Veritas Forum, 2013)
Seven Days That Divide the World (Zondervan, 2011)

Myrtlefield Encounters

Myrtlefield Encounters are complementary studies of biblical literature, Christian teaching and apologetics. The books in this series engage the minds of believers and sceptics. They show how God has spoken in the Bible to address the realities of life and its questions, problems, beauty and potential.

Key Bible Concepts explores and clarifies the central terms of the Christian gospel and provides succinct explanations of the basic vocabulary of Christian thought.
ISBN: 978-1-874584-45-2

The Definition of Christianity throws fresh light on the book of Acts and observes how the first generation of Christians identified and defended the unique features of the gospel.
ISBN: 978-1-874584-49-0

Christianity: Opium or Truth? offers new perspectives on perennial—and crucial—questions such as the problem of pain and the exclusive claims of Jesus Christ.
ISBN: 978-1-874584-53-7

The Bible and Ethics presents a concise survey of leading events and people, ideas, poetry, moral values and ethics across both the Old and New Testaments.
ISBN: 978-1-874584-57-5

In the School of Christ

Lessons on Holiness in John 13–17

Just before his execution Jesus Christ invited his disciples to join him at a borrowed house in Jerusalem to celebrate the Passover. As he faced betrayal, arrest and crucifixion, he taught them about the very heart of the Christian faith, namely, holiness.

When the time came to leave the house, he continued his teaching. As they made their way through darkened streets that were filled with hostility to him, he spoke of how he would empower them to be his witnesses in a world that would often hate them too. Jesus was the teacher; the disciples were his pupils. It was the school of Christ.

David Gooding's exposition reveals the significance of the lessons Jesus taught inside the upper room (chs. 13–14), their connection to the lessons taught outside in the streets (chs. 15–16) and how both parts of this course on holiness relate to the Teacher's prayer to his Father (ch. 17). With a scholar's care for the text of Scripture, he expounds both the devotional richness and the practical nature of the lessons. He shows that to understand Christ's teaching on holiness is to know his power to change lives.

"Of all David Gooding's books this is the one that merits the description 'beautiful'. It is beautiful in its subject matter, as we are privileged to join Mary in 'sitting at Jesus' feet to hear his word'. It is beautiful in its discernment of the structure and contours of the Lord's teaching. It is beautiful in its objective—to create us in the image of the Son of God in holiness."

—**Alec Motyer**, formerly Principal of Trinity College, Bristol

ISBN: 978-1-874584-41-4

True to the Faith

The Acts of the Apostles:
Defining and Defending the Gospel

The Acts of the Apostles is about more than the spread of the gospel to the ends of the earth. By the time the ascended Christ had sent the Holy Spirit to guide his disciples, they had no doubt what the basics of the gospel message were: that Christ died for our sins, was buried and rose again the third day and would one day come again. But, according to Luke's account, difficult questions and challenges arose for the apostles as they began to spread this message. These questions, when once settled by the apostles, would further define the gospel with answers that are definitive for us today.

By carefully tracing Luke's presentation of the historical material, David Gooding shows us that Luke has arranged his historical material into six sections, each containing a set of issues and a dominant question that confronted the church.

"The last time I preached through Acts, *True to the Faith* was constantly at my side. My copy is marked up on every page—some highlighting, some pencil, some ink, different colours of ink, indicating it has been consulted 'divers and sundry' times. With good reason. Gooding not only explains, he stimulates thinking and stirs gratitude. Why any preacher would preach from Acts and not have Gooding at his elbow is beyond me."

—**Dale Ralph Davis**, author, and previously Professor of Old Testament at Reformed Theological Seminary, Jackson, Mississippi

ISBN: 978-1-874584-31-5

An Unshakeable Kingdom

The Letter to the Hebrews for Today

In a clear and concise manner informed by pastoral concern, David Gooding explains the meaning of Hebrews' warnings as he expounds the letter as a whole. He carefully examines the position and temptations of its original readers in the first century. Many were undergoing such severe persecution that they might easily have wondered why, if Jesus really were the Messiah, they had to experience such pain and loss. He expounds its major themes in order to show that its unified message is that hope and enduring faith in Jesus the Messiah, the Son of God, will never be put to shame. As he guides us step by step, he reaches outside the limits of the letter itself in order to explore rich fields of Old Testament history, prophecy, ritual and poetry from which the letter has drawn so many of its insights.

"*An Unshakeable Kingdom* communicates both an inspiring hope and a solemn warning to all those who are following Christ on a journey of faith. This book is written with serious scholarship, penetrating reflection and challenges the reader to uncompromising discipleship."

—**Rev. Dr Patrick Fung**, General Director, OMF International

"What a treasure trove of spiritual riches—gleaned from a lifetime in searching the Scriptures. Read these books, and you will be nourished, stretched, and enlightened, as I was."

—**Dr Lindsay Brown**, International Director of the Lausanne Movement

ISBN: 978-1-874584-36-0

The Riches of Divine Wisdom

The New Testament's Use of the Old Testament

The wisdom of God is revealed in both Old and New Testaments, but it is impossible to appreciate that wisdom fully if the two are read in isolation. Sometimes the New Testament quotes the Old as authoritative. Sometimes it cancels things that the Old says. At other times it indicates that the Old was a type that illustrates New Testament doctrine. How are we to understand and apply its teaching? Is the New Testament being arbitrary when it tells us how to understand the Old, or do its careful interpretations show us how the Old was meant to be understood? Could it be that the New Testament's many different ways of using some of its passages provide us with guidance for reading, studying and applying the whole of the Old Testament?

"*The Riches of Divine Wisdom* is a tour de force. Many Christians fail to take the Old Testament seriously. Others find the New Testament's use of the Old problematic. In this work Professor Gooding offers sane guidance to both groups with eloquence and clarity. He shows how the New Testament itself instructs us in interpreting the Old. Teachers, preachers and all serious Bible students will find it an invaluable resource."

–**Gordon J. Wenham**, Tutor in Old Testament, Trinity College, Bristol; Professor Emeritus of Old Testament, University of Gloucester

ISBN: 978-1-874584-21-6

About the Authors

David W. Gooding is Professor Emeritus of Old Testament Greek at Queen's University, Belfast and a Member of the Royal Irish Academy. He has taught the Bible internationally and lectured on its relevance to philosophy and world religions. He has published scholarly studies on the Septuagint and Old Testament narratives, as well as expositions of Luke, John 13–17, Acts, Hebrews and the New Testament's Use of the Old Testament.

John C. Lennox, Professor of Mathematics at the University of Oxford, is an internationally renowned speaker on the interface of science, philosophy and religion. He regularly teaches at many academic institutions and teaches the Bible extensively. In addition to his academic works, he has published books exploring the relationship between science and Christianity. He has also participated in a number of televised debates with some of the world's leading atheist thinkers.